Le Corbusier and the Tragic View of Architecture

Charles Jencks

Le Corbusier and the Tragic View of Architecture

Harvard University Press Cambridge, Massachusetts

Copyright © Charles Jencks 1973
All rights reserved
Second printing, 1974
Library of Congress Catalog Card Number 73-83422
ISBN 0-674-51860-8 (cloth)
ISBN 0-674-51861-6 (paper)

Printed in the United States of America

To Joseph Zalewski for his insight into Corb

Acknowledgements

In this book, which was contemplated for a long time and written in a short one, I have incurred several large debts of various kinds. I am indebted to Stanislaus von Moos for his marvellous book on Le Corbusier as well as for his friendship and numerous conversations. Others I have spoken to at length about Le Corbusier and those who initially sparked off my appreciation at Harvard University include Eduard Sekler and Jerzy Soltan. Above all I am grateful to Joseph Zalewski – for many revealing midnight conversations. I am also indebted to several people, who either knew Le Corbusier or had written about him, for granting me interviews. These include José Luis Sert, Françoise Choay, Heidi Weber, Peter Blake, Reyner Banham, Erno Goldfinger, Jane Drew, Max Fry, and M. Andrieni at the Fondation Le Corbusier as well as countless others at the Fondation, including Brian Taylor and Paul Turner. I have also been helped by John Donat, Ramsay Short and the BBC, with whom I worked on a television film about Le Corbusier, and by Alvin Boyarsky and his International Institute of Design which sponsored a Corb Symposium. Among those taking part at the symposium I am aware of a debt to Alvin himself, and to Thomas Stevens, Alan Colquhoun, Peter Cook, Paul Oliver, Martin Pawley and Peter Allison – all for their creative ideas and criticisms.

In terms of criticizing my text and offering editorial suggestions, I am indebted to Nikos Stangos and to Pamela Jencks (who have helped me once again), and to the general editors of the *Architect and Society* series, Hugh Honour and John Fleming, whose patience and enthusiasm I regard as fitting rewards for undertaking the whole endeavour.

The translations from French were made by me and corrected by Bernard Tschumi; the reader can check the sources in the footnotes where the French texts are cited. Otherwise I have used the standard English translations, also cited in the footnotes.

Lastly, a special word of thanks to Mr and Mrs Tino Nivola for entertaining me one afternoon in their Long Island garden with a marvellous meal and a series of insights into Le Corbusier's friendly but complex character.

CHARLES JENCKS

Introduction

Le Corbusier is arguably the greatest architect of the twentieth century. Some people, like the critic Lewis Mumford, would reply 'so much the worse for the twentieth century'. Others would raise the question of Frank Lloyd Wright's or another architect's relative merit. But many would accept the assessment. Why? Because of Le Corbusier's undeniable creative potency: he left us a mass of technical–aesthetic inventions which have had a widespread influence on world architecture probably comparable only to Palladio's influence in the past. He changed, or was instrumental in changing, the aesthetic direction of modern architecture twice: once in the twenties with his philosophy of 'Purism' and once in the fifties with his sculptural form of 'Brutalism'.

Beyond these creative contributions, Le Corbusier gave to the modern movement a moral stature and strength which was also quite unique. Recognized as a constant fighter against certain anachronistic tendencies of the academies, or even against an unthinking modernism, he was always looked up to as an uncompromising figure of integrity and conscience, much as Noam Chomsky is now regarded as the incorruptible critic of America's foreign policy, or in the way Alexander Solzhenitsyn is admired for his honesty. (Not surprisingly Solzhenitsyn mentions Le Corbusier's influence in one of his novels.) In large measure this influence was due to Corb's writings – his some fifty books and countless articles – which conveyed a passion and creativity that had a hypnotic effect on a much wider public than any number of buildings could have. The books could be and were translated into many different languages and were not rooted to one place as most buildings are destined to be. Yet his building also exerted a comparable force. As the English architect Peter Smithson put it:

'The German Movement [of Modern Architecture] was rational and severe more than anything else, and in spirit was a continuation of a previous tradition – the ethic of nineteenth-century architecture. It was certainly not one which would make a man leave home and start a new life, which I hold Le Corbusier's work could.'[1]

Indeed Le Corbusier's work did make two or three generations of architects leave home and start a new life – as poorly paid draughtsmen in the

Atelier Le Corbusier at 35 Rue de Sevres, Paris. Young architects came from Poland, Spain, Japan and all parts of the globe to work in his office (located in part of a former Jesuit cloister) and take the message of the 'New Spirit', *'L'Esprit Nouveau',* back home for dissemination. They found their prophet, 'Pope Corbu' as he was later known by detractors, hidden away among his disciples in a tiny, windowless, beautifully proportioned box, sequestered from prying journalists, patiently struggling over the latest project addressed to the new world. In substance many of these projects, city plans, buildings, even paintings and books were naïve if not obviously wrong-headed. The great success of Le Corbusier has brought a concomitant failure and everyone today is well aware that a house is both more and less than 'a machine for living in', that city planning cannot be over-simplified into four different functions and that abstract Purist paintings – no matter how lyrical in their formal relationships – cannot orchestrate the full spectrum of visible emotions.

Precisely because we are living in the aftermath of Le Corbusier's positive contributions, we are also living with their manifest failures which must be acknowledged. Happily, he was honest and outspoken about other people's shortcomings, just as he was frank about his own, so it is permissible to use his own words and honesty against him and yet remain true to his deeper intentions. Basically these consisted in an untiring search after truth – a metaphysical or lyrical truth if not always a scientific one – which ended in a tragic view of the human condition. The presentation of struggle, of his constant battles with the world, was generalized beyond his own personal experience to become the major theme of his life. This book will try to elucidate this view, his personal message, as it is manifest in his architecture, planning, painting and writing.

To concentrate on this theme, as well as his other ideas, I will be quoting more extensively from his writings than would be normal in a book of this nature. When one considers that he produced some fifty books and about fifty-seven finished buildings, one understands the singular nature of his contributions and furthermore the fact that no critic or historian, or more simply, no one at all, has adequately gauged the classification of this work as a whole. It still remains an enigma, to me at any rate. Are we to consider Le Corbusier an architect, or a messianic prophet, or one of the great writers of the twentieth century who couldn't spell and committed all sorts of syntactical outrages? No doubt we should consider all these aspects and more which are clearly evident in his work. Yet this would take me way beyond the confines of a short book and result in a multi-volumed biography, a thing which is beyond the scope of Le Corbusier scholarship at the moment. Perhaps when his private correspondence finally comes to light and the *Fondation Le Corbusier* in Paris publishes his seventy sketch-books a more full and deep analysis can be made. Here I have confined myself to attempting to rethink much of the known evidence in a new light and presenting, whenever possible, new or unusual photographs. The first chapter concentrates on almost completely unknown aspects of his early years in La Chaux-de-Fonds, emphasizing his tumultuous uncertainty which found confirmation and crystallization in the writings of Nietzsche. The second chapter shows where this restless anxiety led: to the formation of a single doctrine which would affect all of modern life. This was presented in four key books on architecture, urbanism, interior design and painting which are discussed together for the first time. The third chapter concentrates on a change in this doctrine, brought about by a sudden interest in women and politics (perhaps the two greatest threats to all doctrines), and the last chapter presents his prolific contributions to new architectural languages. The theme of his Nietzschean, or tragic, view of the human condition runs throughout the book.

A possible point of confusion: since the subject of this book had more than one pseudonym and many nicknames and since I will be intermixing different periods of his life, I will refer to him as Jeanneret up to 1917 and Le Corbusier, or Corb, or Paul Boulard, after that. The exception to this is in his paintings and articles on paintings which continued to be produced under the name Jeanneret until about 1928. The multiple proper names mirror his complexity and elusive character.

Jeanneret's School for Le Corbusier 1887-1916

Charles-Édouard Jeanneret was born on 5 October 1887 in the Swiss watchmaking city of La Chaux-de-Fonds. This city has been, for the last four hundred years, the most important centre for making clocks and watches in the world. Even today it annually exports 44 million watches (nearly half the world production) of a mechanical precision which is unsurpassed. When Le Corbusier wrote *Precisions – The Present State of Architecture and Urbanism* in 1929, he must have been alluding to the meticulous ingenuity of his watchmaking ancestors whose survival often depended on their mechanical ability, for these people were a persecuted sect of French Huguenots who fled to Switzerland in the sixteenth century to establish watchmaking as the major industry of Chaux.

Indeed La Chaux-de-Fonds has always been a haven for political and religious refugees, a fact which is of primary importance in the formation of Le Corbusier's character. He continually spoke of the persecution of his ancestors, the Albigensian heretics, and he apparently was fascinated by the fierce, Manichaean religion of the Cathars with which he directly identified. But La Chaux also attracted such utopian refugees as Jean-Jacques Rousseau, the anarchists Bakunin and Kropotkin, and even Lenin who came to La Chaux and admired its original qualities. What were these?

On a social level, the division of labour into self-sufficient home workshops – in effect the mutual aid and free cooperation of workers' syndicates which anarchists have always seen as the final, liberated state of

1. A Regional-Syndicalist system of Government, 1933, based on power springing from work organizations, or 'métiers', and delegated to a confederation. 'Control' is exerted from below, 'information' from above.

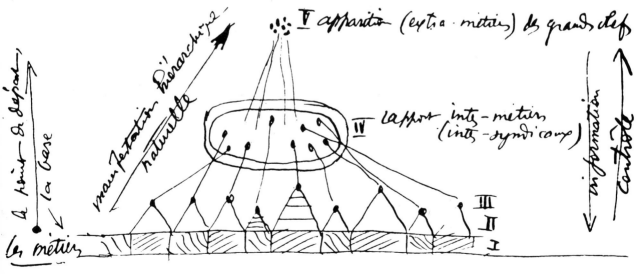

man in society. These already were viable, functioning entities in La Chaux for many years. In 1933, when Le Corbusier was formulating his ideal society for *The Radiant City*, he drew an anarcho-syndicalist form of organization which had parallels with the watchmaking industry of the Swiss Jura [1]. Groups of workmen were to form the true power base of a hierarchical structure where control would be kept decentralized through a representational system.[1] The only way in which this contradicted anarcho-syndicalist theory was in the apex of the hierarchy. Le Corbusier always saw society as being led, if not controlled, by a small group of élite specialists: the great artist and statesman or the 'Captain of Industry', the enlightened businessman.

In any event, La Chaux was a European centre of anarchism in the nineteenth century. When Bakunin split with Marx in 1871, and the working-class movement split between libertarian and authoritarian communism, he settled in La Chaux, found a great response among the watchmakers, and started a political review called *L'Avant-Garde*. The Jeanneret family apparently were among the supporters of Bakunin, and Le Corbusier always spoke with pride of his revolutionary grandparents, of whom one died in prison and another was one of the leaders of the successful revolution of 1848 in La Chaux. The Jeannerets kept alive the tradition of fierce struggle and opposition dating back to their original persecution. A typical family phrase was 'Whatever you do, see that you do it', the words of Rabelais, the motto of Le Corbusier's mother, which he kept as a maxim for life. Looking back in the 1940s at this life of struggle Le Corbusier said:

'Sometimes I despair. Men are so stupid that I'm glad I'm going to die. All my life people have tried to crush me. First they called me a dirty engineer, then a painter who tried to be an architect, then an architect who tried to paint, then a communist, then a Fascist. Luckily, I've always had an iron will. Though timid as a youth, I've forced myself to cross Rubicons. *Je suis un type boxeur.*'[2] [2]

2. Boxing in the hanging Gardens of a collective apartment, 1928. The emphasis on physical sport permeated all Le Corbusier's architecture. Tennis and football were to be played at the foot of every housing block, while running tracks were provided on the roofs.

The fact that tennis courts and football fields and stadia always appeared in his city planning schemes implied more than a belief in the healthy effects of physical exercise. Sport was a type of Darwinian competition which sharpened the individual for his combat with life. In fact Le Corbusier even credited playing basketball in the evenings with giving him the moral security which was reflected in his work! As in ancient Greece, mental harmony and brilliance were to be supported by physical training.

18

At an early age, Charles Jeanneret accompanied his father, who was an expert mountain climber, on many Sunday walks through the Alpine landscapes of La Chaux. These walks were not just feats of physical prowess, but also lessons in seeing, in biological classification, in examining the workings of nature – even its laws.

'That time of adolescence was one of insatiable curiosity. I learned about flowers, both inside and out, the form and colour of birds, I knew how to grow a tree and why it kept its equilibrium even in the middle of a storm.

'My master (the excellent teacher Charles L'Eplattenier) had proclaimed "only nature is inspiring and true and should be the support of human endeavour. But do not make nature in the manner of landscape painters, who show nothing but its exterior. Scrutinize in it the cause, the form, the vital development and make the synthesis of it in creating ornaments." He had an elevated conception of ornament which he conceived of as a microcosm.'[3]

The young Jeanneret made many studies from nature at this time – some were analytic sketches which one could find in biology books, with labels and cross sections, while others were more lyrical drawings of natural forms conceived of as ornament, as rhythmical repetitions and transformations of a single theme [3]. The idea behind these was to find a schematized language of natural form, or *A Grammar of Ornament*, as a book by Owen Jones was called. Jeanneret greatly admired this book, as did so many other Art Nouveau designers, and much of his early work was based on it. For instance an engraved watch of 1902, for which Jeanneret won a prize at fifteen, was in part made up of geometrical,

3 (*left*). **Fir-tree study by Jeanneret, 1905(?),** made under his teacher L'Eplattenier.

4 (*above right*). **Villa Fallet, La Chaux-de-Fonds, 1904–6.** Cubic brackets as rhythmical elements. Jeanneret's brother and mother were musicians greatly interested in eurhythmy and the abstract mathematical nature of music. His early buildings seem like demonstrations of the old metaphor, 'architecture is frozen music'.

5a, b (*opposite*). **Villa Fallet, 1904–6.** This building and the next two show Jeanneret's first attempt to establish a Jura regionalism based on plant forms and such 'Swiss' details as heavy overhanging eaves, steep roofs and picturesque massing.

overlapping planes. When he was persuaded to give up engraving and widen his perspective to architecture, he incorporated this geometricized nature into his first building at the age of seventeen and a half. [4] Already at this time we can find the visual propositions which were to become basic definitions of modern architecture in 1921: 'Architecture is the masterly, correct and magnificent play of masses brought together in light . . . cubes, cones, spheres, cylinders or pyramids are the great primary forms . . . *the most beautiful forms.*'[4] According to Paul Turner, one of the influences behind this abstract Platonic formalism was a book in Jeanneret's possession: Henry Provensal's *L'Art de demain*, 1904. Provensal put forth the idealist arguments that art follows certain absolute laws, that it evolves more and more towards the general and abstract and that beauty is 'The eternal and the general . . . the splendour of truth, as Plato said – It is the quality of the idea reproduced in a symbolic form (Plotinus).'[5] Jeanneret, not surprisingly, bracketed the latter part of this passage in Provensal's book.

However, the attempt to derive a universal language based on a geometricized nature (or classicized Art Nouveau) was only half the question. The other half of Jeanneret's early designs and architecture were concerned with establishing a representative, local form of Art Nouveau

based on the plant and animal forms of the Swiss Jura. In his watch case and first house, already mentioned, he incorporated such organic objects as flowers, a bumble-bee and decorative motifs based on the fir tree [5], [6]. The French Art Nouveau designers, Lalique, Gallé and Guimard, were apparently the inspirations behind this representational regionalism[6] – a form of decorative naturalism which was the first of many alternative modes which Jeanneret was later to reject with emphatic contempt. Imitation followed by partial rejection was his characteristic method of development.

The experience behind the rejection of naturalism and Art Nouveau was his first journey of self-education, a trip in 1907 to Italy, Vienna and Lyon. In Vienna he became acquainted with the ideas of Adolf Loos, more particularly his philosophy being formulated at the time, equating ornament with crime and the idea that only degenerate aristocrats and criminals have need of decorative embellishment. According to the witty arguments of Loos, the enlightened intellectual, as opposed to the uneducated peasant, took his pleasure through the higher, abstract pleasures of Beethoven and hence had no need for distraction through ornamentation.[7] The European intellectual was, supposedly, the end result of cultural evolution. Whereas the primitive savage tattooed his body and had a horror of clean, empty surfaces, more highly developed individuals could forego these cloying distractions for elevated and austere ideals appealing to the mind.

5c (*above*). **Villa Fallet, La Chaux-de-Fonds, 1904–6.** Double glazing is usual in many buildings in La Chaux-de-Fonds. Le Corbusier used this principle later in a new way; see photo [63].

6 (*opposite*). **Villa Jaquemet and Villa Stotzer, La Chaux-de-Fonds, 1908.** Designed while Jeanneret was in Vienna and just before he rejected the formalism of his teacher L'Eplattenier, these two buildings were his last 'Art Nouveau' projects.

PARIS THE WHIP

On this same first journey, Jeanneret encountered individuals who could be seen as Adolf Loos's supreme products of evolution. He visited the Carthusian Monastery of Ema and was greatly impressed by the austere, well-balanced life of the monks, their harmonious equilibrium between individual and collective activities; the cell and the refectory. In Lyon he met an architect who might almost be Loos's new European intellectual. The utopian-socialist Tony Garnier was actually designing a new Industrial City in new materials, reinforced concrete, and a new aesthetic – stripped, whitewashed classicism. When Jeanneret settled in Paris for the year 1908 the effect of these ideas and travels had been assimilated and his transformation was almost complete. He was twenty-one years old and his philosophy and character had been crystallized. This is revealed by a letter to his teacher Charles L'Eplattenier which contains some major themes of his later life – for instance the 'fight with truth itself' as well as the later urgent, passionate tone. It is worth quoting this letter at some length to bring out these points. First is the idea of the modern metropolis, specifically Paris, as a place of Darwinian struggle where one could sharpen one's wits.

'Time spent in Paris is time well spent, to reap a harvest of strength. Paris the immense city of ideas – where you are lost unless you remain severe with yourself. Life is austere and active there. Paris is the crack of the whip at every moment, death for dreamers.'[8]

Later in life Le Corbusier was to think of Paris as cruel, ugly, noisy and chaotic while still being a 'selectioner', a place where genius emerges through incessant competition,[9] a 'place of champions and gladiators . . . Paris is paved with corpses. Paris is an assembly of cannibals who estab-

lish the dogma of the moment. Paris is a selectioner' [7]. The second idea emerges directly from this and concerns the way Paris both destroyed his own romantic dreams and substituted in their place a search for truth and logic. The prophetic note is extraordinary considering his age.

'I have forty years in front of me to reach what I picture to be great on my horizon, which is still flat at the moment. I have finished with childish dreams of a success similar to that of Vienna or Darmstadt [where Art Nouveau formalism then reigned supreme]. I want to fight with truth itself. It will surely torment me. But I am not looking for quietude, or recognition from the world. I will live in sincerity, happy to undergo abuse.'[10]

7. **Sketch of Paris, 1908(?).** Dark, turbulent, threatening forms reminiscent of Edvard Munch characterized Jeanneret's sketches of Paris at the time.

This prediction of struggle *before it actually happened* shows how committed Jeanneret was to a tragic view of the human condition prior to his own suffering. In fact the conflict was built into his destructive–constructive method and it is not surprising to find that Jeanneret was reading Nietzsche's *Thus Spake Zarathustra* at this time.[11] Aside from the similarities in style – passionate, vigorous and aphoristic – there are also similar themes: the 'superman' struggling among men and the necessity that he destroy conventional wisdom before he can realize his revolutionary ideas.

'These eight months shouted to me "Logic, truth, honesty, burn what you loved and love what you burned." The architect should be a man with a logical mind: an enemy of love of the plastic effect; a man of science but also with a heart, an artist and a scholar.'[12]

The ideas are Nietzsche's; almost the words as well. Further on in this letter, Jeanneret described how the architect August Perret had the greatest effect on his conversion, showing him the revolutionary possibilities of reinforced concrete: a new aesthetic, the possibility of a free façade and interior plan through the use of a concrete frame structure, gardens on the roof and so on. Jeanneret also sought an alternative to Art Nouveau formalism in the study of engineering principles such as statics and the strength of materials – all of this rationalism being conceived in moral terms, to toughen the spirit for future battle.

The last major idea to be conveyed in this letter, which also reappeared in later years, was more personal to Jeanneret than the previous two although it also derived from Nietzsche. It concerned the necessarily lonely position of the artist, the necessity for solitude, meditation and almost egotistical creation. He is speaking of the emergent art movement of his friends which sprang up in La Chaux-de-Fonds under L'Eplattenier.

'The movement started too soon . . . the art of tomorrow is an art based on meditation.

'Up the concept and forge ahead! . . .

'[Our youthful friends] did not know what Art is – deep love of one's ego, which one seeks in retreat and solitude, this divine ego which can be a terrestrial ego when it is forced by a struggle to become so. This ego speaks of things embedded deep in the soul; art is born and fleetingly rushes on.

'It is in solitude that one can struggle with one's ego, that one punishes and encourages oneself.

'Our friends must seek solitude. Where? How?'[13]

There are two ways in which these ideas were directly relevant to the later Le Corbusier. For one thing his own creative process took place in isolated spots – an architectural office where he built a little cell, a nine-foot rectangle with blank walls, where he could initiate a project before passing it on to his draughtsmen, or his small cabin in Southern France, another cell-like structure where he worked during vacation [8]. He was to justify isolation, many times, as necessary for supporting a creative élite.

'The man of initiative, of action, of thought, the LEADER, demands shelter for his meditations in a quiet and sure spot; a problem which is indispensable to the health of specialized people.'[14]

8. Petit Cabanon, 1952. The monk's cell placed in a direct relation to nature was an early idea dating from Jeanneret's visit to the Charterhouse of Ema in 1907.

But this need for quietude was also generalized for the whole of society and he traced many social ills to the lack of adequate solitude, citing Pascal. Hence the relevance of isolation to his large architectural projects. In these we always find provision in the house for the individual to be alone, usually in the form of a bedroom, again a 'cellule', or conceptual monk's cell, a place of retreat [76].

GERMAN FUNCTIONALISM

Jeanneret spent the years of 1908-9 working in Paris for Perret and studying in various libraries where he made copious drawings of historical buildings from books. This was a time of consolidation as well as learning. Perret changed Jeanneret's artistic taste, away from the tumultuous Art Nouveau and towards a severe classicism. Jeanneret still admired the Art Nouveau work of the Parisian architect Frantz Jourdain but for its revolutionary use of glass and steel rather than its decoration. Oddly enough, one of the historical periods he copied was the Garden City movement of England, for he later was to reject this. He made direct tracings from journals of the Hampstead Garden suburb. He acquainted himself with the social arguments of Ebenezer Howard and their practical realization by Barry Parker and Raymond Unwin. He even designed a Garden City in a picturesque curvilinear layout for La Chaux-de-Fonds. While soon to reject the aesthetic of pitched roofs and curving streets, he kept an interest in the idea of the industrial city in a park. This led to his early essays in prefabrication and workers' housing: the Domino houses of 1914 and the workers' housing for Saint-Nicolas d'Aliermont of 1917. All this work shows a social concern and interest in mass housing which was rare, although not unique, for its time.

In 1910 there was a further consolidation of his turn towards rationalism and a sober, even Puritanical aesthetic. Jeanneret was sent by the school at La Chaux-de-Fonds to study the evolution of the decorative arts in Germany.

There was a need for a new movement, based midway between art and industry, which would train a new type of craftsman. In his first book, *Étude sur le mouvement d'art décoratif en Allemagne*, published in 1912, Jeanneret set the opposition of art and industry in national terms between France and Germany.

'. . . As French, I suffered in Germany; I was overwhelmed in Paris, where they complained of a German invasion . . . the marvellous Industrial Art of Germany demands to be known . . . Germany is a book of actualities. If Paris is the place of Art, Germany remains the great place of production. Experiences are happening there, the battles are crucial; buildings are raised and the rooms with their historic walls recount the triumph of order and tenacity.'[15]

Jeanneret was greatly impressed with a visit to the architect Peter Behrens, who was in charge of the first large-scale industrial art venture of the twentieth century – designing a whole spectrum of equipment, or industrial products, for the A.E.G. Company. These revealed 'a modest aspect, sober, almost impersonal'. What was later to be known as industrial design and the Bauhaus style was being produced for the first time. Jeanneret also met Walter Gropius and Mies van der Rohe on his visit to Behrens's studio. The other German architects who conveyed the new spirit of functionalism to Jeanneret were Muthesius and Tessenow [9].

9. Project for Felix Klipstein, at Loubach, 1914(?). This villa design shows the influence of Tessenow and Behrens, as does Jeanneret's house for his parents [17]. In 1915, he also produced a design for skyscrapers in a park, another example of the German influence. This is in sketchbook A-2 at the Fondation Le Corbusier; unfortunately they are unwilling to have it reproduced here.

Yet he was not altogether taken in by this new German movement and, in a characteristically dialectical way, argued that functionalism did not necessarily produce beauty and that art was quite independent of utility. This dualism led ultimately to a deepening of his tragic view of the human condition. For, like Nietzsche, he accepted the necessarily opposed conditions of great art: part intellectual and part lyrical, or part Apollonian and part Dionysian. This dualism naturally brought him into continual conflict with other artists and architects because he was actuely aware of the part that might be missing. Hence his attacks on functionalists for lacking poetry and his rejections of Art Nouveau and formalism for lacking rigour. Indeed the conflict between these opposed psychological states was becoming sharp enough in his own mind to set him veering off in yet a new direction. He had absorbed and rejected Art Nouveau and in 1910 he did the same with the nascent German functionalism.

THE USEFUL VOYAGE

Apparently a source behind the latter rejection was a book sent to him advocating a renewed form of Jura-regionalism, Cingria-Vaneyre's *Entretiens de la Ville du Rouet*, published in 1908 and read by Jeanneret late in 1910 when he was still in Germany.[16] According to Paul Turner this book made a new connection for Jeanneret between his area of birth, the 'Suisse-Romande' and classical, Greek culture, for he soon left Germany on an extensive trip, what he called a 'Voyage to the Orient', and then settled in La Chaux for the next six years. The argument proposed in Cingria's book seems strange to someone not acquainted with Swiss culture, but evidently it had a profound effect on Jeanneret. Cingria argued the necessity for creating a local artistic identity for the 'Suisse-Romande', that is the French-speaking part of Switzerland where Jeanneret grew up. The strange aspect of the argument is that this local identity should be Mediterranean in spirit, classical, not northern or gothic; calm, white and made up from right angles. The impact of these meanings is clear in the next few buildings of Jeanneret even if they do not strike us as particularly Swiss or regionalist [**15-20**]. In any event, Jeanneret was convinced that a local Jura revival of culture could occur and that it would be based on Mediterranean classicism. He set off in May 1911 with a young Swiss friend, Auguste Klipstein, on his third journey of self-education to Prague, Vienna, Bucharest, Constantinople, Athens and Florence – among many other cities [**10**]. Jeanneret was twenty-four years old and like many artists at this time in their life, he

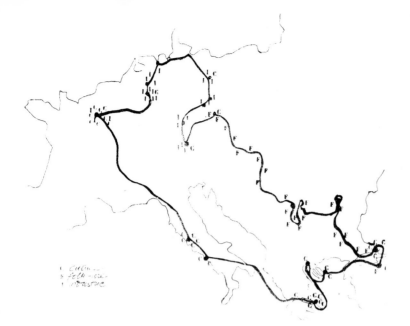

10. 'The Useful Voyage', a map of the 1911 journey classifying Europe into three aspects of civilization: culture (c), folk (f), industrial (i). The passion for classification underlay Jeanneret's self-education and remained throughout his life.

had an urge to travel, to move from one city to the next devouring new experiences and knowledge with an insatiable appetite. He started keeping a sketch-book, a pocket-sized writing pad, to jot down ideas, visual impressions and anecdotes. These sketch-books, of which there are more than seventy covering the whole of Le Corbusier's life, were in themselves a significant addition to Jeanneret's development, for they became a new medium of expression and source book for later ideas. In terms of expression they allowed or forced him to develop a very concise, almost cinematic style of presentation, where ideas, buildings, landscapes and even nude women follow and confront each other in rapid succession. As a source book, they served for later buildings, polemics and paintings. In the self-education of Jeanneret they played a paramount role, a subject which is worth considering for a short time. He said of his first trip from La Chaux in 1907 that self-education gave him a freedom from stereotype and convention.

'I became really appalled at the teachings of the schools, at the set formulas and the assumptions of divine right, and I took it in my head, at that unsettled time, to appeal to my own judgement. With my savings (from my first building), I went on a journey through several countries, far from the schools, and, earning my living in practical occupations, I began to open my eyes . . . When one travels and works with visual things - architecture, painting or sculpture - one uses one's eyes and *draws*, so as to fix deep down in one's experience what is seen. Once the impression has been recorded by the pencil, it stays for good, entered, registered, inscribed. The camera is a tool for idlers, who use a machine to do their seeing for them. To draw oneself, to trace the lines, handle the volumes, organize the surface . . . all this means first to look, and then to observe and finally perhaps to discover . . . and it is then that inspiration may come. Inventing, creating, one's whole being is drawn into action, and it is the action which counts. *Others* stood indifferent – but you *saw*!'[17]

This emphasis on *seeing* what other people only *look at* achieved polemical expression later in *Towards a New Architecture*, with three chapters titled 'Eyes Which Do Not See', devoted to the new aesthetic hidden in ocean liners, aeroplanes and automobiles. The self-educated man can see what others cannot. Yet there are positive disadvantages to being self-taught, especially in the twentieth century. One cannot manipulate ideas very freely, or wheel and deal in concepts as if they were neutral, because each one has come through great effort and is fixed, almost organically, in the mind. The self-taught man tends to be possessive and obsessive with his ideas – he treats them as part of his body. To lose one is like losing a limb. Whereas the academic, or the man who has gained knowledge through books and by training, can deal with ideas more freely, discarding them when they become unfunctional or obsolete. This Le Corbusier had great trouble in doing. In fact in his late fifties, he even regretted his form of self-education.

'I am self-taught in everything, even in sports. And being self-taught, I knew the greatest anguish up to the age of thirty-five. I would not advise anyone to follow the same course.'[18]

In particular, Le Corbusier had trouble breaking away from his fundamental architectural concepts such as the city in the park, or the separating of functions, long after their inadequacies were well known. In most respects, however, his method of learning, at his own pace, and for his own motives, more than made up for a partial inflexibility.

What is quite surprising about the young Jeanneret, and particularly evident at the time of his journey in 1911, is his self-awareness and developed sense of personal identity. This obviously came from his self-education and accounts for the extraordinary feeling of individual destiny which runs through his second book *Le Voyage d'Orient*, written as a series of letters to his artistic friends in La Chaux in 1911 – although not finally published until 1965. Each chapter has the quality of a confession, a testing of some personally held idea. For instance Jeanneret and Klipstein enter into a stormy argument with a Prague student trying to convert him to a new aesthetic based on modern technology.

'We defend beautiful modern technology and say how much all the arts owe to it, in its new plastic expressiveness, its bold realization and its splendid opportunities which offer the builder, from this time on, the freedom from classical servitude. The Hall of Machines in Paris, the Gare du Nord in Hamburg, the autos, aeroplanes, ocean liners and locomotives appear to us as decisive arguments.'[19]

Not only the later arguments for a machine aesthetic are here, but also the same pedagogic and persuasive tone which was to characterize Le Corbusier's subsequent books. Once having discovered some truth for himself and inscribed it in his sketch-book or letter he waited for the opportunity to turn it into a written moral lesson. The major lessons of *Le Voyage d'Orient* were the following.

First, the mosques of Constantinople revealed an 'elemental geometry which disciplined the masses: the square, the cube, the sphere' [11]. Second, the white, simple peasant houses which he found throughout his journey revealed a certain moral rectitude based on a direct harmony with nature. These whitewashed houses were an 'X-ray of beauty . . . an assize court sitting in permanent judgement' on all the objects which were placed against them. Imperfections and visual deceits were quickly exposed by the whitewash. Third, these visual deceits, the eclectic styles which covered or denied the basic underlying functions, were to be found in socially degenerate situations such as the Turkish bazaar, which was not only filthy and noisy, but based on theft, lying and systematic, stylistic fakery. The equation of a decorative revivalism with disease and crime, which Adolf Loos had made, was thus generalized as a kind of economic and moral law. From now on Jeanneret would equate useless consumer objects in all the historical styles, save classicism, with a rapacious form of capitalism. Fourth, it was the monks on Mount Athos, where he spent eighteen days, who revealed the proper attitude towards consumer objects, or the objects of everyday life. The pleasure which they found in basic necessities such as food and drink was manifest in the simplified harmony of the refectory table: the pure forms of wine bottles and dishes conveyed a moral lesson about how little was needed to achieve a relative happiness. It is interesting to note that this moral lesson about the banal objects of everyday use preceded Jeanneret's Purist still-

11. Suleiman Mosque, sketch, 1911.
This pencil sketch, in one of the three styles Jeanneret used at this time, emphasizes both geometrical masses and the great importance of profile or silhouette. Architecture is the play of volumes and the rhythm of light and shadow.

lifes incorporating these objects [24] and his philosophy of 'equipment' which was to show how they could evolve from the industrial process. In fact Mount Athos was to become his view of the good life, a life filled with the poetic presence of basic type-objects; *the* wine bottle, *the* loaf of bread, *the* salami – sun, space and greenery. In countless later drawings of the typical urban apartment we find these basic objects which obviously had a metaphysical presence for Le Corbusier and, in his design for the monastery La Tourette, at least one building where the lesson of Mount Athos was completely realized [105].

The final and most significant lesson of Jeanneret's 1911 journey was learnt in Athens. He describes in *Le Voyage d'Orient* how he stalked the Acropolis a whole day before daring to approach it. He arrived at eleven in the morning, but invented a thousand excuses for not going up to it with his friend Auguste Klipstein. He sat in cafés, drinking and reading the papers, he prowled the streets of old Athens waiting for the sun to set before he launched his direct attack. And when he finally reached it, in the setting sun, when the stone had turned a flaming yellow and orange, he had a strange reaction.

'See what confirms the rectitude of temples, the savagery of the site, their impeccable structure. The spirit of power triumphs. The herald, so terribly lucid, draws to the lips a brazen trumpet and proffers a strident blast. The entablature with a cruel rigidity breaks and terrorizes. The sentiment of an extra human fatality seizes you. The Parthenon, terrible machine, pulverizes and dominates [everything for miles around].'[20]

The Parthenon was seen, oddly enough, as a 'terrible *machine*', a perfected automaton which was cruel and terrifying in its clarity and implacable honesty. It was not until ten years later, in *Towards a New Architecture*, that Le Corbusier spelled out exactly how the Parthenon was a machine. First, it was produced by the same spirit of 'imagination and cold reason' which produced automobiles and aeroplanes, and second, it emerged as a perfected object from technological evolution just as these machines did. It is worth quoting from this later manifesto to clarify ideas which were just being formulated in 1911.

'Every sacrifice, every cleansing had already been performed (by mechanical evolution). The moment was reached when nothing more

12. Photo of the Parthenon, taken by Jeanneret in 1911(?) and published in *Towards a New Architecture*, 1923.

might be taken away, when nothing would be left but these closely-knit and violent elements sounding clear and tragic like brazen trumpets.'[21]

We notice the similar metaphors and the reiteration of the Parthenon as a symbol of the tragic view of the human condition, a conclusion Le Corbusier came back to many times, particularly when he was personally under attack or having inner doubts. The idea of the Parthenon as a machine was elaborated in one more way in 1923.

'We are in the inexorable realm of the mechanical . . . the mouldings are tight and firm . . . all this plastic machinery is realized in marble with the rigour that we have learned to apply to the machine. The impression is of naked, polished steel.'[22] [12]

Whereas the Futurists saw the machine as the alternative to the Parthenon and something which brought noise, dynamism and liberating destruction, for Jeanneret, both the machine and the Parthenon were timeless and silent. They represented ultimate developments which one could return to for 'certainty', as an absolute check against chaotic or changing human affairs. The last quote from *Towards a New Architecture* connects these ideas with a previous one which Jeanneret developed from Loos, Nietzsche and others – that of the great artist, the élite leader.

'It is a question of pure invention, so personal that it may be called that of one man: Phidias made the Parthenon . . . Phidias, Phidias, the great sculptor, made the Parthenon. There has been nothing like it anywhere or at any period. It happened at a moment when things were at their keenest, when a man, stirred by the noblest thoughts, crystallized them in a plastic work of light and shade. The mouldings of the Parthenon are infallible and implacable . . . we are riveted by our senses; we are ravished in our minds; we touch the axis of harmony. No question of religious dogma enters in; no symbolical description, no naturalistic representation; there is nothing but pure forms in precise relationships.'[23]

While these meanings were not precisely worked out until Le Corbusier was about thirty-four, we can still say that at the age of twenty-four he had understood them in general and formulated a basic attitude towards architecture and life: what could be called the 'Parthenon spirit'. Indeed it seems to me that if we are to understand the personal character of Le Corbusier then we will find it most clearly expressed in the meanings which he gives this Greek temple: clarity, precision, implacable honesty, severity, economic competition which produces the perfected machine and the tragic view of the human condition struggling in a hostile universe. It is these meanings which Le Corbusier later introduced into the modern movement and which can be found in his own building – either the reason for their greatness, or the reason for their great failure.

THE NEW ART MOVEMENT

When Jeanneret was in Athens in 1911 he received a letter from his former teacher L'Eplattenier calling him back to La Chaux-de-Fonds. The idea was to form a 'New Section' of the Art School which would cover all aspects of design – from the smallest utensil to architecture – and would stand between art and industry. It was a programme, as Le Corbusier pointed out, similar to that of the later Bauhaus. Jeanneret was put in charge of the architectural training while his friends Georges Aubert and Léon Perrin taught the study of form based on nature (animal, vegetable and mineral objects). Together they formed a team which constructed and decorated such things as small chapels, music rooms and even tombs in the cemetery. The intention was to create a harmonious environment in a unified style, an idea not far from that of the *Gesämtkunstwerk*, or the Art Nouveau idea of transforming the whole environment.

Unfortunately the 'New Section' was not to last for long as a viable institute. From without it was attacked by the conservative bourgeoisie, the other institutes of learning and, to Jeanneret's great shock, the socialists and the socialist-democratic party. Why should this progressive party prove artistically regressive? This contradiction baffled Jeanneret, just as he was later upset by the Communists in 1922. Apparently the socialists felt that teaching artists in industrial matters would produce incompetent half-breeds, ill-trained artists unable to earn a living.

But even within the 'New Section' dissension occurred as Jeanneret and L'Eplattenier fought over the old question of decorative formalism versus a foundation in science, industry and mathematics. 'It is the ruin of all my teaching, it is you who have killed my work of the last ten years,' L'Eplattenier accused Jeanneret.[24] But the bitterness, jealousy and recrimination were more general than this and they became a part of Jeanneret's life in La Chaux for the next five years. When the 'New Section' was finally closed in 1914, he adopted a form of polemic which he was to use whenever a project was thwarted. Along with his friends, he produced a short pamphlet on the event, *Un mouvement d'art à La Chaux-de-Fonds*, with a striking argument in black and white, followed by a supporting testimony of great men: in this case such designers as Hector Guimard in Paris and Peter Behrens in Berlin.[25] This third book of Jeanneret's established his skill as the fighter, the acute dialectician who persuades his audience through a series of violent oppositions. Indeed, Le Corbusier's best books were always set against a powerful adversary, a stupid, evil force to set off his own brilliance and integrity.

The designs and buildings which Jeanneret produced between 1912 and 1917 carried out the synthesis of ideas he had gathered from Perret, Cingria and the voyage to the Middle East. They were often built of reinforced concrete, in a classical style which was seen as specific to the Jura and stripped down to fundamental essentials: doors, windows, arches and pitched roofs. Yet the synthesis was not altogether secure and many inner doubts remained. This can be seen in the revivalist furniture which Jeanneret was designing at the time [13] and in the specifications for 'Louis XIII' and 'Directoire' furniture in his buildings.

When Le Corbusier was later to say 'The "Styles" are a lie,' he was expressing a conviction which came from a great deal of experiment with

13. Design for a Meuble-Secretaire, 1916(?). A revivalist style disciplined by geometry. Geometrical design was the main subject Jeanneret taught in the New Section.

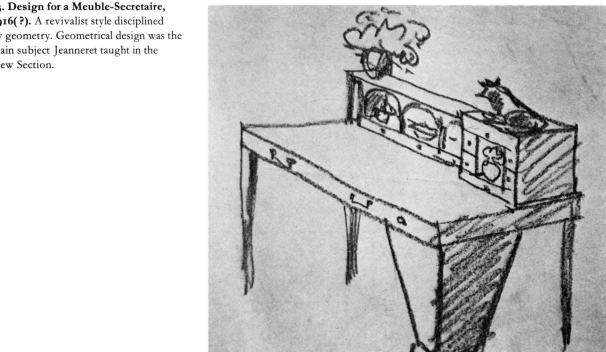

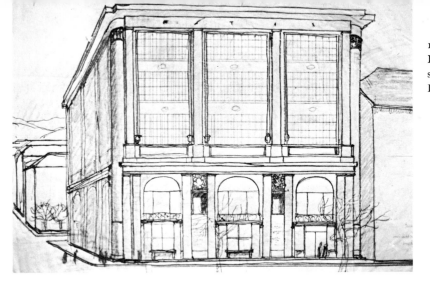

14. Project for a Museum of Beaux-Arts, La Chaux-de-Fonds, 1913. Bi-axial symmetry remained a constant theme of Le Corbusier.

past styles. He had already mastered several of them. Jeanneret's favourites at this time were the Italian Renaissance and what Frank Lloyd Wright called 'stripped or deflowered classicism'. Jeanneret designed a museum in the classical style [14], a house for an industrialist in the Italian villa manner [15, 16] and a house for his parents in the Behrens

15a, b. Villa Favre-Jacot, Le Locle, 1912, These drawings show, as does the house, an integration into the sloping landscape which is reminiscent of Italian villas.

16a, b, c, d. Villa Favre-Jacot, 1912,
views from entry side, hillside and
garden. The capital details were executed by
Jeanneret's collaborator in the New
Section, Léon Perrin.

style of 1910 [17]. It is interesting to note that Jeanneret's clients were all well-to-do and mostly all self-made industrialists. It was this type of client Le Corbusier would later search for, mostly in vain: the great

manufacturer of automobiles, the head of state, the enlightened businessman, or the 'captains of industry'.

Jeanneret himself came from the bourgeoisie, and although he was often destitute and lived like a monk, he kept a certain middle-class style throughout his life. Indeed his starched wing-collar, bow tie and business suit were a sign both of his upbringing and of the polemically held values of anonymity, standardization and precise control [26]. In fact wearing heavy-rimmed dark glasses became, in the *Zeitgeist* of the modern movement, a sure sign that an architect had understood what it was all about. Le Corbusier had shown that the new machine civilization produced a standard architecture which had to be filled with 'object-types' right down to the last standardized button.

Just prior to reaching these conclusions in 1918–19, Jeanneret completed a series of designs which were midway between stripped classicism and the new architecture. His scheme for the *La Scala Cinema*, 1916, was composed of such simple, geometric planes as to be termed by a local paper a masterpiece of a new 'Cubist architecture' [18]. The effect was visually shocking enough to call forth a series of disparaging metaphors – 'it's a warehouse for potatoes, an ice house, a cellar for cheese' – not for the last time such remarks were used against him.[26]

17a, b, c. Villa Jeanneret Père, La Chaux-de-Fonds, 1912. Most of Jeanneret's villas were designed on the outskirts of the city, on the steep slope of a mountain, surrounded by a dense verdure of pine trees. The ribbon window, the strong horizontal cornice, the loggia cut into the centre of a flat white plane, were constant motifs of the later Le Corbusier.

18a, b. Cinema La Scala, La Chaux-de-Fonds, 1916. This striking building contained a forty-foot gallery in reinforced concrete unsupported by columns.

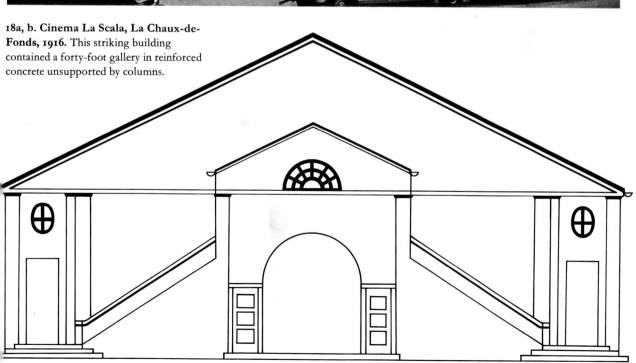

Jeanneret also produced several unbuilt schemes in reinforced concrete which were later to be admitted into the selected *Oeuvre Complète* of Le Corbusier because they illustrated several points of a new architecture. The 'Dom-Ino System' of 1914, a reinforced concrete frame structure, allowed the plan and elevation of the building to be independent of the structure. This naturally led to new aesthetic principles such as the free plan, the free façade and movable partitions. Beyond this the 'Dom-Ino System' contained properties suggested in its name. Like 'Domus' it was intended as housing for post-war reconstruction; like 'domino blocks' it was intended to be mass-produced and assembled in numerous combinations. As a visual concept the 'Dom-Ino System' exerted a strong impact when it was finally published in the twenties because it presented these properties with a beautiful, logical clarity, as if it were some idealized, Platonic essence of the new architecture. In fact the ultra-smooth surfaces often turned out to be costly and inefficient.

Two other schemes of 1916 also used reinforced concrete to achieve a new idealized aesthetic: a house project for Paul Poiret and others [**19**] and a city raised on pylons which established an artificial level above ground separating pedestrians from vehicular traffic. In these two projects Jeanneret started the logical inversion of customary usage for which

19. **'Maison du Diable', Le Locle, project 1915–16(?).** Reinforced concrete transforms the Italian villa into a base for trees; the roof garden emerges from the new technology.

he was later to become famous. Reinforced concrete allows one to have gardens on the roof and, where one is used to finding gardens, on the ground, one finds only clear green space and vehicular traffic.

One completed building, the Villa Schwob, illustrates several of these points and summarizes Jeanneret's development just before he left La

Chaux-de-Fonds for Paris to become Le Corbusier. Like so many of his projects it is a concrete frame villa, one of the first in Europe. It is supported by an independent structure: four interior columns of 20 cm. allow space to flow freely from one room to the next around the central living room [20]. This room, lit from one side by a gigantic vertical

20a, b, c, d. Villa Schwob, La Chaux-de-Fonds, 1916. Views of the exterior and interior, sculptural reliefs by Léon Perrin and several details recall the devotion to geometrical solids reminiscent of Neo-classicism.

window, carries through two stories and acts as the focus for the house. The dining room is to the right, the games room to the left, the stairway behind and the garden in front. The living room is at the centre of a cruciform of space that runs in three dimensions. Not only did reinforced concrete allow this spatial flow, but it also permitted a small flat roof garden and, from a technical point of view, allowed the building to be constructed during the winter when construction usually stops in La Chaux-de-Fonds. The roof and frame were constructed first and then acted as a shelter for further building.

The previous, classical interests of Jeanneret are also evident in the Villa Schwob [21]. There is a clear logical separation between functional zones such as the public ground floor and private rooms above. The rational circulation pattern also follows the best, traditional Beaux-Arts planning. As for the architectural details, they are almost neo-classical in their robust, simplified geometry: blank, flat rectangles, punched into by oval voids, are set off against half cylinders. A pure sphere, as in Goethe's *Altar of Good Fortune*, is poised on a solid flat block.[27] All these geometrical forms are related, in elevation, through a series of 'regulating lines', a method of proportional triangles which Jeanneret used in subsequent buildings to achieve simple relationships between parts. In all this one can see his preoccupation with the idea of mathematical har-

21. Villa Schwob, sketch, 1916. The 'value of profiles' learned from the 1911 journey is rather exaggerated in these gigantic cantilevered cornices.

mony, the Platonic idea that certain fundamental ratios underlie cosmic order and are a cause, if not a sufficient one, of beauty.

In spite of his relative success – seven completed buildings by the age of thirty – Jeanneret felt more and more that La Chaux-de-Fonds was an impossible city for any architect who wished to innovate and create a new architecture comparable to the Greeks in rigour and discipline.

'It seems to me clear that they don't want me any more, because in the end my utter scrupulousness disgusts the people [of La Chaux-de-Fonds]. One has to be conceited, sanctimonious, sure of oneself, swaggering, and never doubting – or at least not let it show. One has to be like a show salesman. *Merde, alors!*'[28]

Jeanneret writes about the incomprehension of his prospective clients, their preferring to remain conventional and banal rather than experiment with new and exciting forms. The provincial nature of Chaux-de-Fonds became oppressive. The Swiss watchmaking town had given Jeanneret several important ideas and commissions, but there was no real opportunity in it for a man bred on Nietzsche and secretly considering himself on a par with Phidias and Michelangelo. In 1917 he was invited by the city of Frankfurt to take part in some municipal building. Just as he received his passport, he decided instead to go to Paris for an indefinite stay.

The Hero of the Heroic Period 1917-28

Jeanneret settled on the left bank of Paris in the Saint Germain des Prés area at 20 rue Jacob. He occupied a kitchen and maid's room on the seventh floor of a Louis XIV mansard apartment for the next seventeen years until he constructed his own apartment in 1934. One of Jeanneret's hopes in going to live in Paris was to start some new mass-production industry based on a new building system such as 'Dom-Ino', and for the next four years he experimented with a series of new masonry technologies. Obviously Perret's success with reinforced concrete was in the back of his mind, because Jeanneret developed one new concrete system after another: a poured concrete method for Troyes in 1919, an asbestos sandwich panel system for the maisons 'Monol' in 1920 and a concrete plus rubble system for the maisons 'Citrohan', also of 1920 [22]. He even started a small brick manufacturing company, which he directed until it collapsed (financially not structurally) in 1921. A series of busi-

22a, b. Maison 'Citrohan', 1920 and Legendre Restaurant, Paris. The standard 'cell' of an apartment block with two blank walls and a double height space. Le Corbusier got the idea for this arrangement from the restaurant where he ate lunch with Ozenfant; he appended the name Citrohan to suggest mass-production, as in the automobile.

49

ness struggles and failures played a great role in sharpening his harsh view of Parisian life and the necessity for discarding romantic conceptions in favour of shrewd, cold calculation.

'A swamp, I found myself in industry. A factory, machines, mass-production, 'cost-price', date of payment, balance-sheets . . . harsh work, in an epoch of economic shipwrecks; shipwrecks everywhere, permanent crises, plunging of statistical curves. It seemed certain that the spirit should be led by a strong discipline . . . a cool reason. Calisthenics of the will. Constitution of a dry judgement. Oh, Bohemian of the Boul-Mich! One does not enter a Bohemian in a stadium of tough competition. It was during these long and serious years that I was keyed up like a tuning fork . . . the why and how of social phenomenon.'[1]

23. Jeanneret, 1921. He lost the use of his left eye when painting his first picture, *The Chimney Piece*, in November 1918.

The photographs of Jeanneret at this time show this effect: a stern, almost glacial expression verging on cruelty, pursed lips, a physiognomy reminiscent of his Calvinist ancestors, an intense gaze [23]. One does not have to be a Marxist to see that Jeanneret's dire economic condition changed his physical one, made him lose weight, and supported his new philosophy of 'Purism' – a doctrine according to which natural selection produces pure forms of elegant, economic simplicity.

Actually, Purism was an aesthetic philosophy first propounded by the painter Amédée Ozenfant in 1916. Ozenfant, born one year before Le Corbusier, in 1886, was the son of the owner of a construction company which used advanced techniques. Through his father, Ozenfant met Auguste Perret, who in turn introduced him to the young Jeanneret. 'He's a very curious bird,' Perret said, 'but he will interest you.' In his *Memoirs*, published in 1967, Ozenfant described, with a slight exaggeration, his influence on this curious Swiss bird, who had the profile of a crow (*corbeau*).

'In May 1917 I finally encountered Charles-Édouard Jeanneret and a new life was to begin for him and me, built on understanding and friendship. We admired both of us equally the masterpieces of modern industry and Jeanneret had a good taste in art, especially ancient, although he was still almost blind in front of Cubism, which made him shrug his shoulders. I initiated him . . . and received a long, moving letter which said . . .

' "All is confusion in me since I started sketching. Throbs of blood push my fingers into arbitrary ways, my reason no longer controls . . . I am disciplined in my actions, but not in my heart and in my ideas. I have let impulses overcome me. In my confusion I think of your clear, quiet willpower. An abyss of time divides us. I am on the threshold of study, you are putting theories into practice . . . Paris, 9th June, 1918 . . ."

'When the war was over, we returned to Paris, I went through a period of diogenism, sold my furniture and moved to the centre of Paris, near the Madeleine Church. The apartment had these gross mouldings with crevices of contorted flowers and ribbons. I wanted to scrape clean these stupidities and whitewash the apartment from top to bottom. This was one of the first signs of the eliminating process in architecture which I called the "Vacuum-cleaning period".'[2]

One is reminded in this passage of Jeanneret's earlier letter to his teacher L'Eplattenier. The two aspects of devotion to a master and destruction of the past are here present. The desire to start life anew with a clean slate, an archetypal urge of the modern movement, was shared by both Ozenfant and Jeanneret. They had a lot in common. Ozenfant had designed the body for a Hispano-Suiza automobile in 1912, in a streamlined classical manner, and he was also fascinated by the new products of industry such as aeroplanes and grain silos. Furthermore, he had also indulged in aesthetic polemics and even run an avant-garde journal, *L'Élan*, from 1915 to 1916. This journal published the Cubo-Futurist artists from Russia as well as the Cubist work from France. It was dedicated to 'France and Art' and stood against the militarism of the 'Bosche'. Aside from a slightly anachronistic nationalism, it was relatively progressive, managing to produce a new, typographical layout which made use of different typefaces and juxtaposed styles. Le Corbusier was shortly to turn this Dadaist typography to his own non-Dadaist ends.

After the 1914-18 war, Dadaism and Cubism were the most creative artistic movements. Purism was seen by its authors as the successor to both. They proclaimed that it would be constructive where Dada was just negative, and rigorously intellectual where Cubism had become decorative. Jeanneret and Ozenfant started painting and writing at night, at a furious pace, and in three months, in November 1918, they published a book, *Après le Cubisme*, and produced an exhibit of Purist paintings. The book, according to Ozenfant, created a great sensation because it was the first published on a new art right after the war. To clinch victory in the struggle of avant-gardes, the authors slipped into a reunion of Cubist painters, where a film on the movement was shown, and surreptitiously inserted at the end of the programme their own extension of the *Zeitgeist*, '*Après le Cubisme*'. This act of psychological warfare had its intended effect – the old guard Cubists were furious.

Among avant-garde manifestos, *Après le Cubisme* was both more polemical and more old-fashioned in its views. It was full of quotations from authors such as Rousseau, Montesquieu and Voltaire. The opening citation from Voltaire set the tone:

'Decadence is produced by facility in making and by laziness in making well, by the satiety with beauty and the taste for the bizarre.'[3]

The authors' main wish was to celebrate the conditions of modern life and persuade both artists and businessmen that they were present at the birth of a positive machine civilization unappreciated by everyone:

'. . . a magnificent epoch, too little understood, often misunderstood, often fought against by artists who ought to root their art in it . . . We have today our Ponts de Gard, we will also have our Parthenon, our epoch is better equipped than that of Pericles to realize the ideal of perfection.'[4]

These references to the Parthenon and perfection show how intent Jeanneret was on making the new architecture an equivalent of ancient virtues.

In the second chapter of the book, titled 'The Modern Spirit' and clearly written by Jeanneret, we find his recurrent interest in the mathematical beauty found in the machine and the Parthenon, and the obsession with classical virtues of strictness and severity. In fact variations on the word 'rigour' recur like a litany. The first chapter on Cubism, probably written by Ozenfant, attacks this movement because of its obscurity, its mystical scientism (all the talk about the fourth dimension) and its lack of representation.[5] In the third chapter, on 'The Laws', the authors state that Purism will recognize subject matter and thus not degenerate into decorative formalism as did its predecessor. They are also led to subject matter because of economic law: the law of natural selection which inevitably produces the pure forms of standardized objects such as the wine bottle, the flask, the pipe, the column. These are the basic '*object types*' we find in the Purists' paintings at this time, even those of Fernand Léger and Juan Gris, which celebrate the 'heroism of everyday life' [24]. For the Purists these rather banal objects had a 'heroic' quality not only because of a certain anonymous dignity and strong restraint, but also because they had been perfected by countless years of re-working. In Paul Valéry's words – 'the best efforts of thousands of men converge towards the most economical and certain shape'.

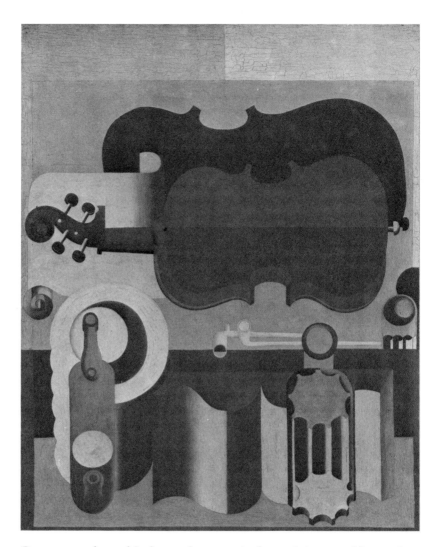

24. Nature morte au Violon, 1920. The geometric profiles of object-types are used to set up a formal symphony. The subject matter, while secondary to form, was important for its universality and evocation of the good simple life.

One can see how this form of economic determinism would appeal to the Calvinist strain in Le Corbusier and how he would next try to find a heroic role in identifying his personal destiny with that of a vast impersonal force. He proclaimed a willing submergence to the industrial process in *Towards a New Architecture*, 1923.

'A great epoch has begun.

'There exists a new spirit.

'Industry, overwhelming us like a flood which rolls on towards its destined end, has furnished us with new tools adapted to this new epoch, animated by the new spirit.

'Economic law unavoidably governs our acts and our thoughts.'[6]

Such sentiments could only be expressed by a man who could animate or personify machine civilization into something like an ideal, living being. Le Corbusier, being an atheist, saw the machine as evidence of a pure cosmic force uncontaminated by personal interference. In this love of the impersonal he was part of a broad international movement extending across disciplines and countries from T. S. Eliot in literature to Eisenstein in film. One quality in what is now becoming known as the 'Heroic Period' of the twenties, in all the arts, was the identification with the impersonal and the universal in civilization. It was this aspect which the doctrine of Purism singled out as its basis.

In 'Le Purisme', an article published in 1921, Ozenfant and Jeanneret tried to establish a universal language of form which would appeal directly to the emotions regardless of education or culture, thus embracing all men. They distinguished two types of formal sensation:

'1. Primary sensations determined in all human beings by the simple play of forms and primary colours. Example: If I show to everyone on Earth – a Frenchman, a Negro, a Laplander – a sphere in the form of a billiard ball (one of the most perfect human materializations of the sphere), I release in each of these individuals an identical sensation inherent in the spherical form: *This is the constant primary sensation* . . .

'2. There are secondary associations, varying with the individual because they depend upon his cultural or hereditary capital . . . Primary sensations constitute the bases of the plastic language: these are the *fixed words* of the plastic language . . . it does not seem necessary to expatiate at length on this elementary truth that anything of universal value is worth more than anything of merely individual value. It is the condemnation of "individualistic" art to the benefit of "universal" art.'[7] [25]

Jeanneret's attempt to find the 'fixed words' of an artistic language are surprisingly like his first searches in Art Nouveau [3] and his last attempts to establish a formal language based on natural symbols, as at Chandigarh. Throughout his life, Le Corbusier was searching for a type of universal symbolism that would be trans-historical and non-conventional. Like so many sons of the Enlightenment, he never came to terms with the idea that perhaps convention itself might be universal. To him it meant pettiness, provinciality, subjectivity and snobbism – all the things that the Beaux-Arts' convention of classicism entailed in the twenties.

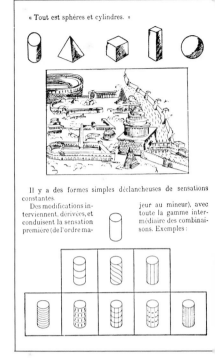

25. **Page illustrating Purisme from L'Esprit Nouveau.** The 'fixed words' of the plastic language are presented like propositions in a French school book on geometry.

It was against these meanings that the review *L'Esprit Nouveau* was launched by Ozenfant and Jeanneret in October 1920. Basically a call to order in its title (which was borrowed from Apollinaire's writings), this monthly magazine proclaimed the new, international spirit on every page. This was partly due to the fact that the two editors wrote most of these pages themselves – under various pseudonyms. Ozenfant disguised himself as Julien Caron, Saugnier, Vaucrecy and de Fayet, whereas Jeanneret occasionally wrote under the latter two names as well as Le Corbusier, Paul Boulard and even ***! It was like some nineteenth-century revolutionary sect where everyone had a pseudonym in case they were caught by the police. Just as 'Lenin' and 'Stalin' were adopted personae which were invented for practical reasons, and then swallowed the original men, so was 'Le Corbusier'. Ozenfant described the genesis of this persona.

'I wished to keep my real name Ozenfant for articles on painting and aesthetics in general. For architecture I will take the name of my mother: Saugnier. Take that of your mother . . .

– Impossible, she is a Perret! Like Auguste!

– Well then, take that of a cousin . . .

– We have the Lecorbésier (or Lecorbézier), who are happily all dead . . .

– Good, you will revive the name, you will be Le Corbusier in two parts, which will make it richer!'[8]

Other less publicized reasons for the pseudonym Le Corbusier were Jeanneret's profile which resembled a crow (*corbeau*, which he used as his insignia in letters and drawings) and various sexual overtones to the last part of the pseudonym. It is significant, or at least appropriate, that the article 'Le' preceded the name because it gave a certain objective stature to the persona, as if Le Corbusier was himself some object-type or *'homme-type'*, perfected by thousands of years of economic history. Indeed the persona allowed Jeanneret to write about himself in the third person as 'he' or 'our man did this' as if he were some universal witness suffering the course of twentieth-century history for all men. The pseudonym was at the same time a protective mask and a means of self-dramatization. It had similar overtones to his other inventions such as the Citrohan house or *brise-soleil*: something to be accepted as a basic fact of modern life. 'Le Style Corbu' became known around the world as a synonym for the new architecture. Today in Marseille when one tries to

26. Ozenfant and Jeanneret on the Eiffel Tower, 26 June 1923. Two 'hommes-types' in their standard dress.

find the Unité d'Habitation one has no luck, until one says, 'Where is the Le Corbusier?' The persona became a household word conjuring up as many precise meanings as IBM and Xerox were to signify in the sixties.

Most of the articles on architecture appearing in *L'Esprit Nouveau* were signed 'Le Corbusier-Saugnier' to signify that Le Corbusier did the writing while Ozenfant supplied the photos and some of the ideas. Their joint articles on painting were signed Ozenfant and Jeanneret, opposed to an alphabetical ordering, to signify who was most responsible for the argument in these cases. Inevitably, however, confusions and jealousy became rampant and the two parted in bitterness in 1925, the year *L'Esprit Nouveau* stopped publishing. Le Corbusier was furious that Ozenfant should change dates on several paintings to prove that Ozenfant always had an idea a year earlier. Also 'Saugnier' was getting too much credit for having written *Towards a New Architecture*, which was published in 1923 under the hybrid name, immediately achieving worldwide fame. So Le Corbusier omitted the name Saugnier from the second edition and dedicated the book to Ozenfant. 'The fellow thanked me for the dedication . . . he didn't realize that by printing it I had prevented anyone from thinking he'd written the book.'[9] Ozenfant, for his part, complained that the joint signature caused a number of people to believe that he had a mistress called Le Corbusier. He gave a small cheque to Le Corbusier for his services on the magazine – so paltry a sum that Le Corbusier kept it in his pocket for the rest of his life to pull out whenever he needed to discredit his former friend.

Yet for seven years the two were almost inseparable cohorts in their fight for a new sensibility appropriate to the modern age [26]. The similarity and breadth of their outlook allowed them to establish an avant-garde review which was diverse in subject, while unified in attitude. Basically the same message, the heroic potential of modern life, came across in articles on music, literature, philosophy, psychology, economics, painting, sculpture, architecture and politics. The 'New Architecture' of Le Corbusier-Saugnier was complemented by an article by Dr Pierre Winter on 'Le Corps Nouveau'. A renovation of body and mind was called for, illustrated by Isadora Duncan-like figures leaping across purified objects in Greek garb. Albert Jeanneret, Le Corbusier's brother, wrote articles on eurythmy and advertised his school on it in the magazine. A continuous theme was sounded in all the issues: 'a great epoch has begun. There is a new spirit: it is a spirit of construction and of synthesis guided by a clear conception.'

Issues of *L'Esprit Nouveau* reached the Bauhaus in Weimar and students immediately called for an alternative to the Expressionism then prevailing there: 'machines for living in' instead of 'glass cathedrals of the future'. In Moscow, the emergent Constructivist movement saw Le Corbusier as a herald of their new society, not only because of his slogan emphasizing 'a spirit of construction', but also because of his communal housing schemes [27]. In 1924, the Constructivist architect Moses Ginz-

burg wrote a book called *Style and Epoch* and sent a dedicated copy to Le Corbusier-Saugnier. The book is not only composed like *Towards a New Architecture*, but also contains the same polemical illustrations of grain silos, aeroplanes and ocean liners. Ginzburg was the major creative force behind collectivist housing in Russia and became a close friend of Le Corbusier when he visited there several times in the late twenties (one of the few western architects to do so).

It would be an exaggeration to claim that Le Corbusier was mostly responsible for the 'Heroic Period' of Modern Architecture. Certainly Theo Van Doesburg and De Stijl in Holland provided much of the impetus, as did Constructivism in Russia and the Bauhaus in Germany. Yet if any one architect is to be singled out, and it would be awkward to have a heroic period without a hero, then it would have to be Le Corbusier – for his self-conscious moral position as much as his buildings. The classical hero in Western culture is an individual who sees the major problems confronting society, sees them rationally, and then acts directly to change them. Furthermore, he is morally and personally involved in this action in a way which is different from those who are part of a move-

27. Freehold Maisonettes, 1922.
Stemming from Le Corbusier's interest in the Charterhouse of Ema in 1907 and his Citrohan house, this project became a model for the communal houses constructed in Russia in the late twenties. Communal facilities like kitchens and gymnasia were provided, while each individual apartment had its private garden like the monks of Ema.

ment or *Zeitgeist*. He takes all mistakes and setbacks as a personal responsibility, thus suffering where others would claim immunity. Perhaps Le Corbusier got some of these ideas from Nietzsche's notion of the superman; at any rate he had a highly developed sense of his own destiny.

'This is a successful achievement, to be able to say to oneself: "I want to attain a certain end, and I shall leave no stone unturned. I shall wait for the proper moment. I shall succeed in what I have decided to do. I shall arrive at the chosen time, at the proper place, calm and smiling, a conqueror and not a casualty." Real heroes are well groomed and absolutely controlled. They are neither unshaven, nor unkept, nor blood-stained. The gods themselves smile.'[10]

It is generally understood by Le Corbusier's admirers that he was relatively un-bloodstained, or, as they phrase it, he didn't bother himself with petty squabbles, attacking other architects and indulging in destructive polemics. This view is profoundly false and fails to take into account the eminently dialectical nature of his argument. For every positive point, there is someone or something which is destroyed. In later life Le Corbusier was partly embarrassed by this fact and apologized for attacks on a sculptor he had admired when very young.

'A thousand excuses for the wickedness done to Rodin . . . But "Paul" [the blasphemer] was at the age of revolt and discovery . . . He burned what he loved.'[11]

The 'Paul' who Le Corbusier is apologizing for here was of course another persona, 'Paul Boulard', who had carried out the Nietzschean injunction to burn what he loved in order to create something totally new and superhuman – in this specific case the machine aesthetic.

Before outlining the positive creations of Le Corbusier which established his role in the Heroic Period, it is worthwhile considering his destructive side, not only because it is vitually unknown, but also because it was so complete, up-to-date and it evinces a feeling of joyful struggle, a love of attack. Under his various pseudonyms, such as Paul Boulard, he attacked not only the École des Beaux-Arts, but De Stijl, Constructivism, Gropius and the Bauhaus, Expressionism and Surrealism. Unlike most artists, he had to criticize a competitive movement before he could assimilate its lessons.

In *L'Esprit Nouveau* between 1921 and 1924, Le Corbusier condemned all modern German architecture for being based on error: 'Appearances'.

'In architecture such an error is fatal. The systematic use of the vertical, in Germany, is a mysticism, a mysticism of physical law, the poison of German architecture. The Germans wished to make their architecture one of the most active armaments of pangermanism ... the German embassy in Saint-Petersburg, the factories of A.E.G. in Berlin, are conceived to impose, to crush, to cry out absolute power.'[12]

This attack on Peter Behrens, an architect whom the young Jeanneret had worked for and admired, was not only against the monumental nationalism, but also against a supposedly false technology, verticality, as opposed to Le Corbusier's technically determined horizontal buildings.

'A simple fact condemns everything: in a house one lives floor by floor, horizontally not vertically. The German palaces are just lift cages. Here is the aesthetic of caskets.'[13]

The argument which Le Corbusier continues to bring against the Germans is their lack of technical rationality. Gropius and the Bauhaus are wrong (in 1923) because they teach decorative art and not architecture or research into standardization which Le Corbusier was pursuing.

'But what saddens us is the obligation to have to conclude that a school of art has the absolute incapacity to ameliorate industrial production, to create standards: one cannot invent standards out of the blue. For a long time, in this grave question of teaching, we have concluded that the schools of applied art must be closed, because we cannot admit the industrial product removed from the standards, we cannot admit the objects of decorative art. Now the Bauhaus at Weimar brings nothing to industry, but just creates decorators who are superfluous and undesirable quantities ... we desire exact objects ... There thus exist many schools to be closed.'[14]

Le Corbusier's, or rather Paul Boulard's, greatest wrath is directly against German Expressionism, the architecture of Hans Poelzig, which resembles the ruins of Rome, and of Hermann Finsterlin which resembles 'viscous ejaculations recalling underwater horrors'.

'In the depths of our being, larva, toads and beasts which haunt the memories of the primordial world re-emerge again today ... we see them in this new crisis of the spirit which followed the war: frightening dreams of Hermann Finsterlin from Bavaria [28] with their viscous ejaculations recalling underwater horrors, or those viscera, or impure

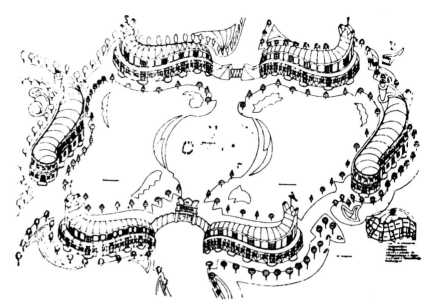

acts of beasts. He was pretending to extract out of this architectural creations ... Bruno Taut ... publishes in his review houses where one finds the same distracted neurasthenia. But physical matter is against it. These things can be born in a fevered head and inscribed on paper. Physical facts refuse to let them be built.'[15]

This last statement was of course factually untrue as Le Corbusier showed by illustrating Mendelsohn's Einstein Tower, an Expressionist building which influenced his own Ronchamp thirty years later [88]. Yet in dialectical terms, proving Expressionism unbuildable was necessary in order to prove his own architecture to be generated by constructional laws. The Constructivists, in this dialectic, were the antithesis of Expressionism, but still only one more erroneous solution on the way to true synthesis.

'Here is the mirage: *the poetic attitude of truth perceived on the base of geometry is not so easily a plastic truth.* Russian Constructivism makes this jump too quickly, too much without considering pure, plastic facts; things are misunderstood! Still it's very seductive and incomparably better than the hell of Finsterlin! It's as much in the truth as the others are in error. Antipodes. It's at the antipodes of neurasthenia.'[16]

Elsewhere Le Corbusier faulted the Constructivists for thinking that art had nothing more to do than resemble machines, again forgetting that there were certain aesthetic laws, based on pure forms, which were eternal. The De Stijl artists who based their work on these laws still suffered for not taking real objects as their point of departure. And the Surrealists, who are praised for having understood that real objects have a natural poetry and beauty, are nevertheless criticized for thinking that these objects are either banal or the result of elevated dreams. When they are beautiful, industrial objects are functional and real (not surreal). 'The realist, useful object is beautiful.'[17] This thesis is next countered by an antithesis when Le Corbusier moves to attack the German functionalists.

Thus, Le Corbusier moves from one attack to the next, always changing the criticism to suit his ends. It is a game he cannot lose, as is all dialectic wielded by a clever duellist. What's the point? For one thing each attack is justified in so far as it goes, and for another it crystallized a stage in his own positive development. The extremes of abstract art led to the Purist insistence on the industrial object; the monumental German nationalism led to anonymous, internationalist housing projects. Beyond this progress through opposition, there were the unique qualities of relevance and commitment.

Le Corbusier (unlike other architects such as Gropius, Wright or Mies van der Rohe) always stayed in touch with and alert to the contemporary issues. When the issue happened to be a reactionary, rightist nationalism, he wrote a book, *Croisade*, condemning it (while the other architects remained silent or indeed collaborated); when there was a reaction of the younger generation against the new establishment, including himself, he saw its point. Being always *engagé* with the present situation had its limitations, but it did serve to keep Le Corbusier creatively acute right up until his death at the age of seventy-eight in 1965. He never stopped enjoying a good fight and the youthful vitality evinced in levelling all opposing contenders was as much a part of *L'Esprit Nouveau*, the new, heroic spirit, as anything else. What it brought about, naturally, was counter-attack and a life lived more as a warrior than a gentleman. But this is what is asked of heroes and it would be unfair to expect from them images of domestic bliss and comfort. A lot of the criticism of Le Corbusier's buildings stems from this misunderstanding, or from the unwillingness to accept the new, spartan way of life for which they are designed and which they so poetically imply.

This positive programme for a reformation of life was set out in four key books written between 1921 and 1925: *Vers une architecture*, *Urbanisme*, *L'Art décoratif d'aujourd'hui*, and, with Ozenfant, *La Peinture Moderne*. Such creative output was phenomenal considering also the

29. Pavilion of L'Esprit Nouveau, 1925. Various views of the revolution proposed for modern living: purist paintings on the wall; industrial 'equipment' instead of interior decoration; a prefabricated cell with 'hanging garden'; a collection of cells with communal services forming a superblock. Le Corbusier wrote a book explaining the four different revolutions which would occur as a whole – a modern *Gesamtkunstwerk*.

buildings he produced at the time. Le Corbusier wrote about 10,000 words a month during these crucial five years with *L'Esprit Nouveau*, and like a good journalist turned author, he made every shot count twice by turning all the articles into books of several different languages. The four books, which reproduced articles from *L'Esprit Nouveau* in their original form and size, gave the impression of a *total* change in life inasmuch as they covered architecture, urbanism, industrial design and painting. Like his Pavilion of the New Spirit [**29**], finished in 1925, the same year in which the last three books were published, they covered a spectrum of interests from the door knob to the regional plan – all

from the same attitude. Hence the overpowering feeling they give of the *Zeitgeist* moving through every aspect of modern life. In purely polemical terms the four books were far more persuasive than other architectural manifestoes published in the twentieth century and they deserve to be studied in their own right, as contributions to a literary genre which has only recently flourished. No doubt they owe something to biblical and political tracts, to Nietzsche's aphorisms and Marx's masculine reasonings, to the artistic manifestoes of Apollinaire and the Futurists. But their combination of styles and ideas go beyond all these. In form they consist of short chapters introduced by an 'argument', in blank verse, which is reiterated throughout the text so persuasively that one forgets to note both its dubiety and illogicality. The arguments are supported by newspaper cuttings, textbook illustrations of such unlikely subjects as bidets and monkeys playing guitars, photos of astrophysical

30. Page from *L'Art décoratif d'aujourd'hui,* in the chapter on 'The Spirit of Truth'. Other images of Truth in this chapter include sea-shells, Santa Sophia, aeroplanes, fighters, gunboats, cross-sections of plants, asteroids, comets and a dirigible.

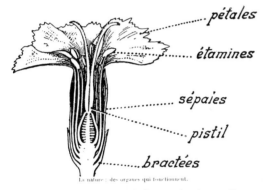

pétales
étamines
sépales
pistil
bractées

La nature : des organes qui fonctionnent.

quelques espèces. Les lois de la physique astreignent ces systèmes à des aventures rigoureusement fatales.

Destinées, causes, raisons? Mystère; ce n'est pas notre affaire.

La nature et l'événement sont étrangers à notre force créatrice: ils sont en dehors, il leur arrive de se mettre au travers. Mais dans ce qui concerne notre œuvre, le travail humain, l'organisation humaine, le monde humain, rien n'existe ou n'a le droit d'exister qui ne soit explicable. Nous nous mettons au travail : tout doit être clair, car nous ne sommes pas des fous. Nous travaillons ayant un but... si bête puisse-t-il être.

La nacelle d'un dirigeable.

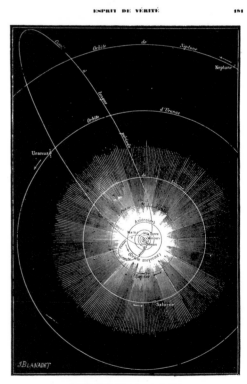

ESPRIT DE VÉRITÉ   181

J. BLANADET

Ce qu'on sait des faits qui nous entourent.

discoveries, pencil drawings and sometimes even missing photographs (which the reader is meant to supply with photos of up-to-date equipment). The juxtaposition of typographical styles and subject matter, the argument through poetry, anecdote, statistics and biblical rhetoric have all had an effect on twentieth-century journalism from *Time* magazine to Tom Wolfe. The argument conducted through photographs and captions has influenced the former, whereas the baroque – telegraphic – neo-hysterical style has, in some way, come through to the latter. Since the specific arguments of the four books had such a profound effect on modern architecture and what became known as the International Style, a summary of them is appropriate here, linking them up with Le Corbusier's buildings produced at the time.

Towards a New Architecture

As already mentioned, by 1911 Le Corbusier had come to several important conclusions which were to be given final articulation in the twenties: in essence the Parthenon spirit, the idea that the Parthenon was an absolute in civilization, both a machine which had been perfected through evolution and a symbol of the tragic human condition. His other major conclusion was that architecture is basically an art of geometric volumes or 'the masterly, correct and magnificent play of masses brought together in light'. These two ideas were given seminal formulation in *Vers une architecture*, 1923, and supported by various related ideas which could be termed, in general, mechanical, social and metaphysical.

The mechanical idea concerned first of all 'the engineer's aesthetic' and more importantly the engineer's morality of unblinkered truth, as opposed to the deceits of the then current architecture. As usual, the argument proceeds dialectically, with the noble savage engineer pitted against the 'obsequious', 'peevish' architect.

'A QUESTION of morality; lack of truth is intolerable, we perish in untruth.'[18]

One of the truths which the engineer, as opposed to the architect, upholds is that of only preserving useful tools and scrapping all others:

'We throw the out-of-date tool on the scrap heap; . . . this action is a manifestation of health, of moral health, of *morale* also; it is not right that we should produce bad things because of a bad tool; nor is it right that we should waste our energy, our health and our courage because of a bad tool; it must be thrown away and replaced.'[19]

The idea of utility, or functionalism, is not, however, a *sufficient* cause of architecture and it is extended in several ways. First it is accepted as a departure point, a necessary condition for architecture, because of its idealistic, even Platonic qualities.

'We claim in the name of the steamship, of the airplane, and of the motor-car the right to health, logic, daring, harmony, perfection.'[20]

Qualities which some engineers may strive after, but only those who have a prior, cultural commitment. Next, this supposedly radical functionalism is modified by the introduction of emotional and metaphysical values.

'The purpose of construction is TO MAKE THINGS HOLD TOGETHER: of architecture TO MOVE US. Architectural emotion exists when the work rings within us in tune with a universe whose laws we obey, recognize and respect.'[21]

Later on we find, as with Plato, that the language which is common both to us and to the universe is based on geometry, pure mathematical ratios and ultimate truths.

'This sounding-board which vibrates in us is our criterion of harmony. This is indeed the axis on which Man is organized in perfect accord with Nature and probably with the Universe . . . this axis leads us to assume a unity of conduct in the universe and to admit a single will behind it. The laws of physics are thus a corollary to this axis and if we recognize (and love) science and its works, it is because both one and the other force us to admit they are prescribed by this primal will . . . If the canoe, the musical instrument, the turbine, all results of experiment and calculation, appear to us to be "organized" phenomena, that is to say as having themselves a certain life, it is because they are based upon that axis. From this we get a possible definition of harmony, that is to say a moment of accord with the axis which lies in man, and so with the laws of the universe – a return to universal law.'[22]

Not surprisingly the Parthenon is the supreme example of an object which is basically functional and still made up from universal harmonies that are 'in accord with the axis which lies in man'. If the mechanical and metaphysical arguments have been slightly Platonic, then the supporting social ideas are even more so. For Plato's élite of philosopher kings we get a modern substitute of enlightened businessmen.

'We are all acquainted with too many big businessmen, bankers and merchants, who tell us: "Ah, but I am merely a man of affairs, I live entirely outside the art world, I am a Philistine." We protest and tell them: "All your energies are directed towards this magnificent end which is the forging of the tools of an epoch, and which is creating throughout the whole world this accumulation of very beautiful things in which economic law reigns supreme, and mathematical exactness is joined to daring and imagination, that is what you do; that, to be exact, is beauty." '[23]

Later in *Vers une architecture*, this élitism is developed in Fascist directions (a very good friend of Le Corbusier at this time was the French Fascist Dr Pierre Winter).

'The art of our period is performing its proper functions when it addresses itself to the chosen few ... Art is not an essential pabulum except for the chosen few who have need of meditation in order that they may lead. Art is in its essence arrogant.'[24]

Or:

'The social contract which has evolved through the ages fixes standardized classes, functions and needs producing standardized products.'[25]

Or:

'Rome's business was to conquer the world and govern it.'[26]

Finally in the last chapter, called 'Architecture or Revolution', we see a synthesis of these élitist ideas as the enlightened businessman is equated with the great artist and the managerial élite, or perhaps what we would call today the technocrats.

'The magnificent flowering of industry in our epoch has created a special class of intellectuals so numerous that it constitutes the really active stratum of society ... the engineers, the heads of departments, legal representatives, secretaries, editors, accountants ... The modern age is spread before them, sparkling and radiant ...'[27]

An example of such an enlightened businessman was Le Corbusier's first major client in Paris, the Swiss banker, Raoul La Roche, who not only commissioned this radical new architecture but also bought the new Cubist and Purist paintings around which the house was designed

[31]. The display of these paintings accounts for the fact that part of the house is an 'architectural promenade', i.e. a controlled sequence of spaces, commencing with a triple height entrance hall and, depending on the route, ending either in a ramped gallery or an open-air roof garden. The spatial sequence is truly remarkable and remained a constant preoccupation of Le Corbusier. In the entrance hall we find over-

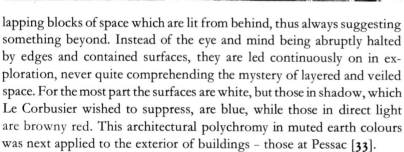

lapping blocks of space which are lit from behind, thus always suggesting something beyond. Instead of the eye and mind being abruptly halted by edges and contained surfaces, they are led continuously on in exploration, never quite comprehending the mystery of layered and veiled space. For the most part the surfaces are white, but those in shadow, which Le Corbusier wished to suppress, are blue, while those in direct light are browny red. This architectural polychromy in muted earth colours was next applied to the exterior of buildings – those at Pessac [33].

The City of Tomorrow

The fifty-one workers' houses built in Pessac, a suburb of Bordeaux, constituted one of the largest schemes Le Corbusier was to build, and hence can be appropriately connected with his next book *Urbanisme* (or *The City of Tomorrow* as it was somewhat misleadingly titled in English

**31a, b, c, d, e. La Roche-Jeanneret
House, Paris, 1923,** in its present state
now the *Fondation Le Corbusier*. Various
comparative views, 1925 and 1971. The
curved gallery contained Le Corbusier's
first use of the ramp. Note the way a
continuation of space is implied by the
lighting and layering of punched-out
flat surfaces.

– Le Corbusier always denied being a futurist and called it *The Contemporary City*). This book develops certain earlier ideas, some forcefully, some to the point of absurdity.

The first three chapters attempt to show that a rectilinear geometry is not only functional, for speed, and beautiful, because clear, but the basis of the best culture as well. 'Culture is an orthogonal state of mind' is one of the absurd epigrams which typifies much of the argument, just as does the opening statement:

'Man walks in a straight line because he has a goal and knows where he is going; he has made up his mind to reach some particular place and he goes straight to it. The pack-donkey meanders along, meditates a little in his scatter-brained and distracted fashion, he zigzags . . .'[28]

This chapter ends, not surprisingly, with the conclusion that because of winding roads 'cities sink to nothing and ruling classes are overthrown'. The whole argument culminates in a view of civilization reminiscent of Vitruvius and Vasari: namely the idea that there are contrasting periods of civilization and barbarity – which can be known by the *style* of life and which are in some sense cumulative developments. For Le Corbusier, the barbaric disequilibrium of curved lines, jagged surfaces, and unclear decoration is inferior to the classical equilibrium of rectangles and pure volumes – 'One is a symbol of perfection, the other of effort only.' Behind these questionable views were two interesting ideas: first, the Purist concept that certain forms constitute a natural language, and second, that classicism was a natural result of modern industry.

'This modern sentiment is a spirit of geometry, a spirit of construction and synthesis. Exactitude and order are its essential conditions . . . In the place of individualism and its fevered products, we prefer the commonplace, the everyday, the rule to the exception . . . a general beauty draws us in, and the heroically beautiful seems merely theatrical. We prefer Bach to Wagner, and the spirit that inspired the Parthenon to that which created the cathedral.'[29]

In part this argument had a certain plausibility inasmuch as most engineering work was geometrical and classical and the modern sensibility which does emerge from anonymous city life tends to prefer 'Bach to Wagner', or everyday objects to revivalist ones. But combined with his social arguments, this leads to the following kind of absurdity.

'Thus a street which had one uniform cornice seen against the sky would be a most important advance toward a noble architecture. If we could insert such an innovation on the agendas of town councils, we should be adding enormously to the happiness of the inhabitants. We must always remember that the fates of cities are decided in the Town Hall; municipal councils decide the destinies of town planning.'[30]

The idea that one could change people's lives through architectural form never really left Le Corbusier, but the idea that architecture was political was dropped by the end of the book.

'My role has been a technical one . . . since the Russian Revolution it has become the charming prerogative of both our own and the Bolshevist revolutionaries to keep the title of revolutionary to themselves alone . . . [my "Contemporary City" of 1922] was severely criticized [by the Communists] because I had not labelled the finest building on my plan "People's Hall", "Soviet" or "Syndicalist Hall" and so on; and because I did not crown my plan with the slogan "Nationalization of all property".

'I have been very careful not to depart from the technical side of my problem. I am an architect; no one is going to make a politician of me.

' "A Contemporary City" has no label, it is not dedicated to our existing Bourgeois-Capitalist society nor to the Third International. It is a Technical work . . .

'*Things are not revolutionized by making revolutions.* The real Revolution lies in the solution of existing problems.'[31]

Thus Le Corbusier emerges now as the apolitical technocrat, the neutral doctor solving society's problems no matter what the ideology. And yet certain definite social forms *are* favoured. The 'Contemporary City' has the business élite at its centre. This consists of twenty-four glass skyscrapers containing offices rather than, say, a town hall or cathedral, which occupy the centres of most 'ideal' plans [35]. Throughout *Urbanisme* there are many references to the 'Captains of Industry' which show that Le Corbusier was looking to business for the new meritocracy and there are many appeals for a new town builder to emerge, such as Louis XIV or Colbert, who is capable of making a clear, grand decision to build the city at a stroke.

Le Corbusier found such a patron, on a small scale, in M. Henri Fruges, an enlightened industrialist who had inherited a sugar-cube factory from his father. When Fruges commissioned Le Corbusier to build the white, box-like workers' houses at Pessac, not surprisingly they were compared to sugar-cubes. At any rate, Fruges was, like so many of Le Corbusier's clients, an altruistic, creative businessman who had read his writings and been persuaded by the idealism.

'I am going to enable you to realize your theories in practice – right up to their most extreme consequences – Pessac should be a laboratory . . . standardization and mass-production.'[32]

Here was a 'Captain of Industry' engaging in intelligent, good works, here was a 'Louis XIV capable of saying "We wish it" or "such is our pleasure"' – the ending words of *Urbanisme*.

M. Fruges was not only a benevolent industrialist but he described himself as an 'explorer, multivalent artist, architect . . . painter . . . sculptor, pianist and composer, member of S.A.C.E.M. of Paris, writer, art critic, historian, etc. . . .'[33] It probably took such a man to commission Le Corbusier to construct workers' housing as an altruistic experiment.

In any case, it is significant for Le Corbusier's social arguments that such a man took an interest in his idealistic proposals and continued to do so. For these arguments are based on an unusual form of idealistic paternalism or liberal élitism or Fascist benevolence. They all tend towards the conclusion that a few great men lead society towards its own best interest, or that social liberation and health can only be achieved through the action of the few. It is not surprising that Dr Pierre Winter, in an article of praise, justified Pessac as the new architecture for Fascism: it combined a new order with cheapness, health, rationality and clarity. Just as Mussolini's Fascism combined mass social reforms with a new technology, all led by an élite, so did Le Corbusier's Pessac.

In fact Pessac was built from standardized elements used in ever-changing combinations [32]. This was not just an economic or technical

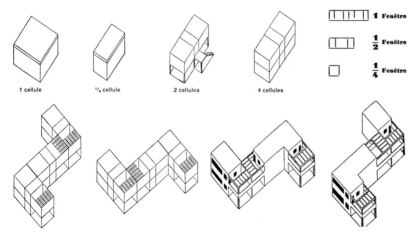

1 cellule   ¹/₂ cellule   2 cellules   4 cellules

☐☐☐☐☐ **1 Fenêtre**

☐☐☐ **½ Fenêtre**

☐ **¼ Fenêtre**

32 (*left*). **Pessac, 1925.** The basic elements of construction consist of the basic cube, or cell, the reinforced concrete beam of 16 feet 3 inches, and the ribbon window. **33** (*opposite*). **Axonometric View of Pessac, 1925.** A mixture of high and low buildings placed at different angles yet all built from similar elements. The verdure which separates these buildings is also dispersed in different ways. All this led the inhabitants to consider the area less monotonous and oppressive than a comparable modern development.

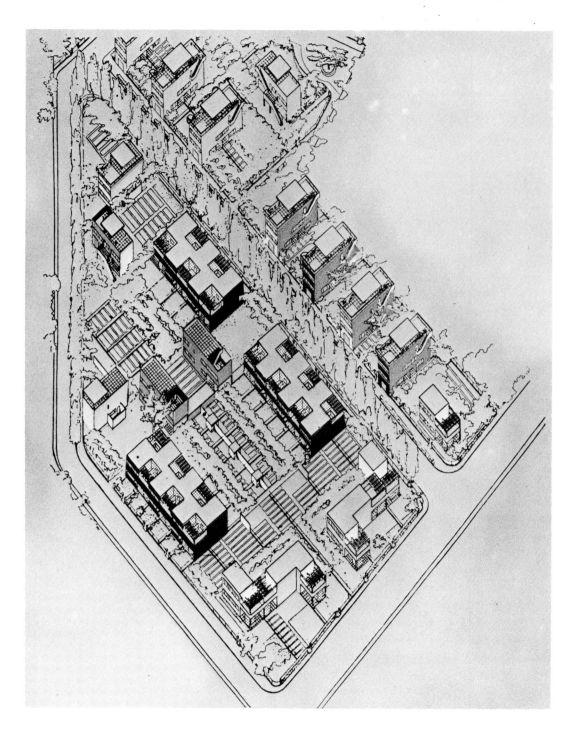

decision, but also an aesthetic one. As Le Corbusier said in *Urbanisme*, quoting the eighteenth-century French classicist Abbé Laugier:

'1. *Chaos, disorder, and a wild variety in the general layout* (i.e. a composition rich in contrapuntal elements like a fugue or symphony).

'2. *Uniformity in detail* (i.e. reticence, decency, "alignment" in detail).'[34]

Pessac has this very interesting combination of similar detailed elements making up ever different ensembles [33]. The elements are intermixed in such an elaborate way that they never become dull or predictable as in most mass housing. Furthermore they are mixed with verdure to create an ambiguous whole of trees, walls and columns, 'where there is no inside or outside' of the environment – another lesson of *Urbanisme*. Perhaps Le Corbusier's best-known urban idea at this time was the 'City in the Park', the idea of achieving urban densities along with the benefits of nature by building high or with complex setbacks. At Pessac, we find nature introduced by intricate methods such as setbacks, gardens and tree-lined axes. This also gives a sense of identity to a building task, workers' housing, where it is rarely found. Indeed, judging by the sociological study which Philippe Boudon has carried out on Pessac,[35] we can see that it comes rather close to Le Corbusier's vision of the Charterhouse at Ema: an ideal resolution of individual initiative and collective well-being [34].

While such collective elements as windows, staircases, heating equipment and kitchen were standardized, and thus achieved economies, they were assembled in rather non-repetitive ways and left with flexible, open space. Hence the inhabitants have used these 'standards' in all sorts of individual ways, walling up ribbon windows, filling out terraces, dividing up the open-plan rooms, etc. This has, of course, destroyed the visual consistency of the architecture – a point which Le Corbusier enigmatically answered – 'You know, it's life that's always right and the architect who's wrong.' An ironic answer, intended to be so. Just as a 'house was a machine for living in', it was also a poetic ruin of crumbling concrete and primitive masonry. Just as Le Corbusier's 'standards' were machine-tooled objects of Platonic perfection and precision, they were also rough stones, trees and a bottle of wine. Starting with the idea of resolving two incompatibilities like the individual and the group, it was not surprising that Le Corbusier could end up, as at Pessac, by admiring the way personalization was destroying his own architecture. All the arguments for a geometrical civilization, put forward in *Urbanisme*, were countered by the 'barbaric' actions of the inhabitants at Pessac,

74

34a, b. Pessac, 1925 and 1969. The vast alterations which this workers' housing has undergone extend much beyond the visual changes. The open planning of Le Corbusier has allowed for many changes in use and construction – a very flexible personalized architecture as it has turned out.

and yet, according to the supreme dialectician, these barbarians were still 'right'.

The final ideas which Le Corbusier develops in *Urbanisme* concern the actual functioning of 'A Contemporary City' and it is here that he emerges as a neutral technologist. Most of these ideas are connected with transportation around the slogan 'a city built for speed is built for success'. Basically, he divides up different speeds and types of traffic, and puts them on different levels so that they can cross without interference. We find, in section, a complex Futurist City with all sorts of traffic interpenetrating and even, like the Futurists, a suicidal airport located in the centre of office towers. The functional motives behind a 'A Contemporary City' are four: to de-congest the city centre, increase density and circulation, and create more open, green space. The forms which result from these motives are straight lines and right angles interspersed with flowing irregular greenery [35]. It is rather like the standard *Beaux-Arts* city plan with radial axes and symmetrical gateways, *Arcs de Triomphes*, surrounded by a green belt and eaten into, on one side, by English landscape gardening (which was to be the area reserved for future expansion). The 'brains', the businessmen, were in the centre in their cruciform, sixty-storey glass and steel towers of omniscience. To the left were their

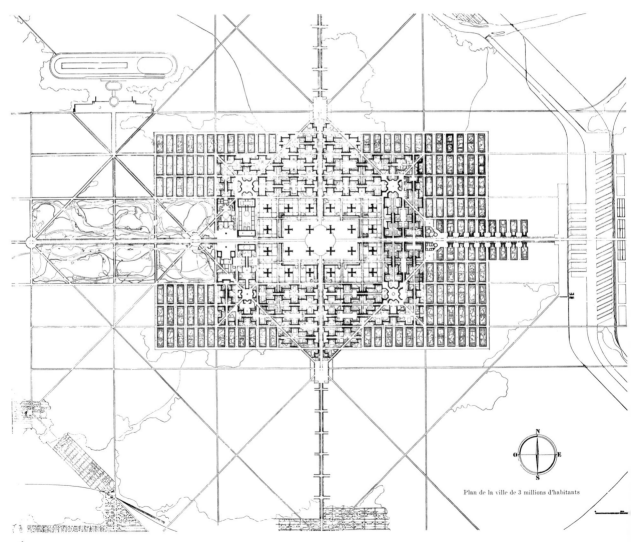

Plan de la ville de 3 millions d'habitants

cultural institutions, to the right their industry. Above and below the business centre two different classes of worker were housed: one in indented blocks of commodious apartments, the other in lower super-blocks of freehold maisonettes [27]. This built-in class distinction supervised by a managerial élite of businessmen had certain affinities with corporate Fascism even though Le Corbusier denied any political commitment or ideology. In a sense, it is the apotheosis of an idealized business world where *harmony* was to be achieved through economic competition, not exploitation or conflict. Everybody was to gain, even through the method of finance. Thus the urban land would be redistributed, foreign capital would be attracted for investment in new buildings, and the increase in land values would pay for profits for everyone.

In this benevolent pragmatism we can see Le Corbusier's hope (which he shared with other liberal architects like Gropius and Mies) of escaping from conventional political thinking and alternatives. When CIAM (*Congrès Internationaux d'Architecture Moderne*) was formed in 1928 it put as one of its main points a theory of land reform which straddled many political positions and was no doubt written by Le Corbusier.

'This redistribution of the land, the indispensable preliminary basis for any town planning, must include the just division between owners and the community of the *unearned increment* resulting from works of joint interest.'[36]

In other words, one would redistribute the land (communist), but one would still have owners (capitalist), plus an increase in profit due to larger densities (pragmatic) which would be divided equally between owners and the community (capitalist, anarchist). It is not surprising that Le Corbusier and CIAM were accused of every political sin in the book. Their apolitical politics consisted in trying to do all positive things at once, without having bloodshed, class war or an erosion of freedom – an outcome which if pragmatically difficult was nonetheless desirable.

L'Art décoratif d'aujourd'hui

The same kind of optimistic positivism can be found in Le Corbusier's next book, *L'Art décoratif d'aujourd'hui*, also published in 1925. In this he discusses three cataclysms brought about by the machine: the industrial, social and moral revolutions.

'There already exists, and it will increase, the consequences of the crisis which separates the pre-machinist society from the new machine

35. **A Contemporary City, 1922–5.** Some of the main ideas presented polemically by this plan were the separation of the four basic city functions, the separation of vehicular and pedestrian traffic, the super-block, and the city in the park raised on pilotis or stilts.

age society. Culture has taken a step and hierarchical decoration is crushed. Gilt is erased and the slums will not wait to be abolished. It seems that one is working in the establishment of a simple and economic *human scale* . . . The palace of the single man no longer exists. Pageantry has left Aubusson (tapestry-making) and is elevated now into the mind. The worker's house already occupies a few beautiful and healthy spaces, and the bathroom enters into everyday usage; first class in the métro differs from second only by four sous; the bus stop is a democratic place where men both in bully's cap and top-coat queue up; taking off his cap, the man says with security, "Sir, can I have a light please?" '[37]

This ideal of social liberation, obtained through the machine, was shared by many artists of the time, for instance those of De Stijl. They saw that the machine's large-scale effect was to re-align institutions along functional rather than class lines and that machine production tended to be antipathetic to conventional decorative forms of hierarchical display. The whole of *Decorative Art Today* (never translated into English) was devoted to proving that decorative art couldn't exist today and that artists and architects must search for its contemporary equivalent: 'equipment' or standardized, industrial objects which had their own type of beauty. This beauty resulted from a pure search after function and, if the search was successful, objects which were as clear and aesthetically pleasing as the laws of nature, geometrical bodies, seashells and all visual manifestations of cosmic truths. However, much of Le Corbusier's argument is spent in putting these objects in their place - a position of restraint and discretion *below* that of great Art, a place in the background where they won't usurp attention, where they can function unnoticed as silent, dutiful servants.

'Decorative art is an imprecise term by which one represents the whole of human *object-members*. These respond with a certain exactitude to ordered needs which are clearly objective. Need-types, function-types, therefore object-types and furniture-types. The human object-member is a docile servant. A good servant is discreet and self effacing to leave his master free. Decorative art is equipment, beautiful equipment.'[38]

Throughout his books, Le Corbusier gave countless examples of the new equipment which modern life had created: 'its fountain pen, its eversharp pencil, its typewriter, its telephone, its admirable office furniture, its plate-glass and its 'Innovation' trunks, the safety razor and the briar pipe, the bowler hat and the limousine'.[39] Aside from a functional beauty which was anonymous, this equipment also had the advantage that it set a standard based on the human scale.

'When the typewriter was invented, typing paper was standardized; this standardization had a considerable repercussion on furniture, it established a module, that of the commercial format . . . this format was not an arbitrary measure. Later, one appreciated its wisdom (the anthropocentric measure) which it established. In all objects of universal usage, individual fantasy recedes in front of the human fact.'[40]

Le Corbusier follows this with a list of common, anthropomorphic dimensions which typing paper supposedly introduced into many different areas such as books, photography, magazines, etc. Although parts of the argument could be disputed, its overall import was undoubtedly true: utilitarian objects of everyday life introduced a relative anonymity and standardization based on human dimensions. This has found recognition today in the fields of industrial design, ergonomics, anthropometrics, Le Corbusier's own 'Modular System' and a host of sciences which study basic human measurements and relative standards. As in *Towards a New Architecture*, the morality consists in scrapping objects when they cease to function:

'Useful objects of our existence have liberated more slaves than heretofore. They are themselves the slaves, the valets and servants. Would you take them as confidants? One sits on them, one works on them, one works in them, one works them: once used they are replaced.'[41]

But again, pure utility is not the only criterion to be considered and, in this first chapter (titled *'Iconologie, Iconolatres, Iconoclastes'*) Le Corbusier argues for an iconology which is *appropriate* to its subject. The ostrich plumes of Louis XIV were appropriate to his role as a despot, whereas their use today by courtesans, antiquarians and professors is an anachronism. Contrary to this is appropriate iconology.

'Lenin was seated in the Café La Rotunda on a cane chair; he had paid for his coffee twenty centimes, a tip of one sou. He drank with a small cup of white porcelain. He wore a bowler hat and a brilliant and sleek collar. He wrote away the hours on typewriter paper. His ink-stand was sleek and round, made of bottle glass.

'He prepared himself to govern a hundred million men.'[42]

The implication was that correct iconology might conquer the world, like Lenin. And yet today, Le Corbusier argued, decoration was being misused by almost everyone: to deceive and flatter, to distract people in their loneliness, to impress social snobs and to camouflage basic mistakes. His teacher Auguste Perret had said, 'Decoration always hides a mistake in construction'. Proceeding dialectically, Le Corbusier opposes to the camouflaged dandy the 'ALL NAKED MAN'.

'The all naked man does not wear an embroidered waistcoat; he wishes to think. The all naked man is a person who is normally conditioned, who has no need of tinsel foil . . . He does not worship fetishes. He is not a collector, he is not a museum conservator. If he likes to instruct himself, it is to arm himself. It's to equip himself to attack the tasks of the day. If he likes, in his time, to look around and behind himself, it is to seize the "why" of things. And encountering harmony, that which is a creation of his spirit, he receives a shock which is moving, elevating, encouraging, which gives him a support for life.'[43]

This 'all naked man', obviously the ancestor of Loos's ornament-less intellectual, sustains himself not on the myths and religions of the past, but on the new, industrial folklore of popular science and cosmology.

'Cinema, books [and magazines such as] *Je Sais tout, Science et Vie,* have replaced by their documentation all the poetics of yesterday. The mystery of nature, which we attack scientifically and hardly exhaust, always grows deeper and more profound the more we advance. In fact it becomes our new folklore. The esoteric symbol, we still have, for those initiated today, in the curves which represent forces, in the formulae which resolve natural phenomena.'[44]

Here we have the kind of complete revolution in daily living and metaphysics which was to make up *L'Esprit Nouveau.* The modern urban man, the all naked man, was to nourish himself on a diet befitting both a monk and a scientist, an athlete and scholar. The 'equipment' which Le Corbusier designed to fill out this daily life inevitably had overtones of the laboratory, hospital, gymnasium and monastery. These were the metaphors which counted, the metaphors of truth.

With the aid of a very young and attractive girl, Charlotte Perriand, Le Corbusier designed a series of chairs, tables and built-in cupboards which were meant to furnish the modern apartment. These have an elegance and attention to the contrast of fine materials, such as calf-skin with chrome, that show the presence of a feminine sensibility. In fact Charlotte Perriand remained a very close friend of Le Corbusier for the rest of his life, only breaking off intimate contact in the early forties when she and Pierre Jeanneret went into the Resistance while Le Corbusier worked for Vichy. Except for this break, which was later healed, she remained one of the *'fidèles'*, those loyal friends whom Le Corbusier characterized with such key-words as *'brave-type'*, *'solide'*, *'costaud'*.

The work on the 'equipment' started in 1927 and culminated in an exhibition room designed for the *Salon d'Automne* in 1929 [36]. As in all

36. Salon d'Automne, 1929, with Charlotte Perriand. Storage walls of chrome, glass, mirror and back-lit translucent plastic divide up the space and contain the 'clutter' of possessions.

his work, Le Corbusier starts from basic functional requirements which he takes to be constant and universal. In this case they are the basic postures of the human body and basic, daily activities such as reading, talking and reclining. From these requirements, or 'object-members', he derives the 'object-types' or 'standards': the easy chair for reading and relaxing, the *'basculant'*, a reworking of the British Officer's chair, for active discussions and 'demonstrating a thesis', and the form fitting *chaise-longue* for reclining [37]. Not surprisingly these three chairs are modern versions of older prototypes. Since the intention was to find the standard and perfect it, this was to be expected. It is interesting to see how Perriand and Le Corbusier have extended the inherent metaphors of each prototype. For instance the traditional easy chair of the club and the gentleman's library, the *grand confort*, becomes more heavy, plushy, squashy and orotund. It has five bulging, black, rectangular cushions squeezed up by thin glistening chromium tubes. These tubes embrace, even pinch, the cushions, offering them up to the human bottom as the essence of 'grand comfort'. The *basculant*, with its pivoting backrest, is as taut as a bow; in fact its leather arm-rests are strung tightly by springs. The basic division, as in all the chairs, between heavy structure and body support is kept, with the former being articulated in chrome tubes, the latter in calf-hide. Visually and conceptually we have a basic separation of functions. The overall feeling is of delicate fur being suspended within a frame of precise machinery, 'a chair is a machine for sitting in' being Le Corbusier's explicit metaphor. In fact, this particular machine can be physically painful if one makes the wrong move and activates the pivoting backrest. On the other hand, the *chaise-longue* is very comfortable, being moulded in shape to the reclining posture. The softened Z-shape, a very sculptural form which gives a feeling of embrace, is underlined by the continuous flowing line of the chromium tube, a reworking in metal of effects previously obtained in bentwood. Because this Z-shape is further supported at four points by a sub-structure, the metaphor becomes one of offering up the reclining body for sacrifice or display. It is as if the body is being propped up on fingertips like a precious jewel. The ostensible function of the sub-structure is to allow for different reclining positions.

In the case of the standard storage wall the intention has been to provide a thick movable partition which zig-zags in section so that it can be used from both sides and so that it can liberate the house from clutter – rather like Japanese storage space built from screens. In the 'Manual of the Dwelling' (1923), Le Corbusier states his case for cleanliness and purgation with a pugilistic kind of irony.

'Demand bare walls in your bedroom, your living room and your dining room. Built-in fittings to take the place of much of the furniture which is expensive to buy, takes up much room and needs looking after . . .

'Demand concealed or diffused lighting.

'Demand a vacuum cleaner.

'Buy only practical furniture and never buy decorative "pieces". If you want to see bad taste, go into the houses of the rich. Put only a few pictures on your walls and none but good ones . . .

'The true collector of pictures arranges them in a cabinet and hangs on the wall the particular painting he wants to look at; but your walls are a riot of all manner of things.'[45]

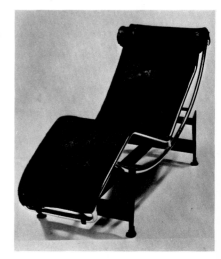

La Peinture Moderne

This selective attitude towards art brings us to the last of four related revolutions proposed by 1925, *La Peinture Moderne*, written with Ozenfant, under his original name Jeanneret. In this book, many of the previous arguments of Purism are extended and given final formulation.

37a, b, c (*opposite*). Three chairs, 1927-9, with Charlotte Perriand: *grand confort, basculant* and *chaise-longue* are in production. **38 (*below*). Nature Morte de L'Esprit Nouveau, Jeanneret, 1924.** Numerous objects superimposed in side elevation and plan like an engineering drawing. The rectangular geometry and regulating lines discipline the whole, giving a very static and calm feeling. These are the 'higher', more 'intellectual' emotions to which the Purists appealed.

For instance the idea that mechanical evolution leads at once towards the universal and the geometrical culminates in the slogan that 'man is a geometrical animal'.

'His spirit has created the geometry; the geometry responds to our profound need to order. The works which move us the most are those where geometry is perceptible.'[46] [38]

In this light nature is seen as a rather imperfect artist, 'disorderly in aspect', who realizes greatness only in happy moments when he accidentally produces such perfect bodies as the crystal.

'The spirit of man and nature find a factor in common, an area of agreement, in the crystal just as in the cell, where the order is perceptible to the point where it justifies the human laws of explaining nature which the reason has been pleased to impose.'[47]

This jumble of ideas, this linking of empiricism and rationalism, is interesting in so far as it shows the authors' intention of basing art on science. An almost scientific determinism is advanced, reminiscent of today's McLuhanism, to prove that there can be only one type of modern sensibility conditioned by the new technologies.

'Steel has revolutionized society' and created an environment where everything is based on the right angle; therefore man has to be a geometrical animal. Photography, cinema and the press have rendered the need for representational art obsolete: stories can now be told better in other media, while art can concentrate on its own ends of being a pure, *emotional* language. Modern life, with its basis in science, measurement and exactitude, has created a new superior breed of man, whose reason reigns supreme, who is more complex and intelligent, and who achieves the highest state of development – self-knowledge.

'We understand for want of a better word, by *Hieratism*, the state of the mind which a civilization reaches when, leaving the empirical period, it becomes conscious of that which previously it only felt . . . *Hieratism* is the age of knowledge, knowledge of itself, moment of knowledge acquired after a long period of research. It is thus the moment when man is no longer pushed about by exterior forces or by pure instincts and is in a position to guide himself and choose among the technical means those which permit him to satisfy his spiritual needs of this new intellectual state . . . when Egyptian priests had their hieratic types sculptured they knew that what was being fabricated was a machine to provoke sacred emotions.'[48]

The authors insist that this new, Nietzschean man does not look for beauty or pleasure in art, but rather character and emotion.

'. . . as it was put, the problem of beauty was insoluble. *The error at its basis was to give as a criterion of beauty the idea of pleasure, a final reaction altogether personal and variable* . . . judgement varies with each individual . . . all discussion based on the worth of a work of art was thus vicious . . . the Parthenon is not pleasurable to anyone. Great art is not art of agreement . . . art has the sole duty to move us . . . The Parthenon moves everyone powerfully, even those whom it displeases; what counts is the intensity of the provoked emotion.'[49]

Finally, to complete the argument for a determined, modern sensibility, the authors put forward another nineteenth-century idea which Matthew Arnold, as again Nietzsche, had proposed.

'[Modern man] has need of the ideal certainties which previously religion gave him; doubting it now and metaphysics also, he is driven in on himself where the true world goes on within; the anguishing emptiness which nothing can fill ... except art ... Art will have the mission of superior distraction and it will give this exalted contentment without which the calm of the soul is impossible.'[50]

Art and culture as the substitute for religion obviously gave these pursuits a function, or exalted importance, which they could not adequately fulfil, and it was just after this formulation that both Ozenfant and Jeanneret gave up what amounted to their Purist religion and returned to more nourishing subjects. Jeanneret's painting had become academic and rarefied. By 1928 he introduced 'objects evoking a poetic reaction' into his painting – specifically the female form – and not coincidentally, became more interested in women. Before turning to this next stage in his life, it is appropriate to conclude the Purist development with a discussion of his two buildings in which it culminated: the villas at Garches and Poissy near Paris.

TWO IDEAL VILLAS

Both villas were constructed for wealthy, enlightened clients, who had connections with both art and industry and who hence could be seen on the one hand as élite 'captains of industry' and on the other hand as those with an acute self-knowledge: collectors of the most modern art. The villa at Garches, 1927, was inhabited by Gertrude Stein's brother, who built part of the street-car system of San Francisco and whose wife was one of the first collectors of Matisse. The Villa Savoie at Poissy, 1929-31, was built as a luxurious weekend retreat for clients who, according to Le Corbusier, had no preconception as to what a new architecture could be. It would be claiming too much to say that these clients would have subscribed to the philosophy of *Hieratism*, but at least Le Corbusier could see them as examples of the modern sensibility in its different aspects.

In formal terms, the two villas can be seen as abstract cubes of space in which various geometric elements are freely disposed as in a Purist painting. The three-dimensional grid, this Cartesian coordinate system, exists as an ideal order throughout the buildings even where elements are left out or filled in over the column and floor grid. The idea, developed from the 1914 Dom-Ino System, gave birth to several new principles which Le Corbusier partially enunciated as the 'Five points of a New Architecture': the house on stilts or *pilotis* which frees the ground for circulation; the roof garden allowed by the flat roof; the free plan and façade allowed by the independent frame structure; the ribbon window which gives more light than that in the load-bearing wall.[51] In addition to these innovations, there are several characteristic elements,

39. Archizoom, No Stop City, A Climatic Universal City, 1970. Several elements such as structure and services freely composed in an endless Cartesian space – an extension of Le Corbusier's urban planning of the *Ville Radieuse*.

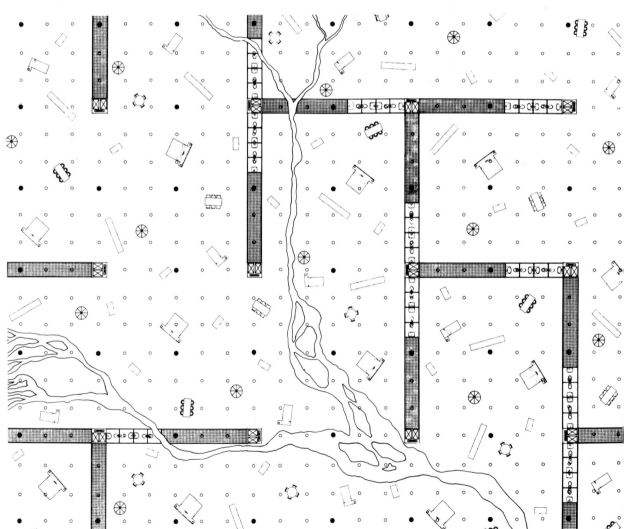

found in these two buildings, which Le Corbusier would often compose in abstract space: the ramp or bridge, the double-height space, the scissor and spiral staircase; the curved bathroom or curved solarium (a tertiary space). One might consider these nine elements of a new architecture as comparable to the *object-types* in a Purist painting. They are invented for both their technological and aesthetic potential and then used as fixed words in an abstract system of Cartesian space. This idea can perhaps best be seen in its most recent, extreme form, the 'No Stop City, A Climatic Universal City' by the Archizoom Group in Florence [39]. These designers have taken Le Corbusier's Platonic approach to its limit and imagined a continuous grid in a space extending everywhere in the world and filled with perfected, beautiful servicing elements. The difference, if there is any, is that Le Corbusier smashes his elements into and through each other to produce what I would call 'compaction composition' [40], whereas Archizoom leaves the elements separate. Thus in Le Corbusier's architecture, holes of space are cut violently through floors, columns are placed very close to walls, curved partitions jut into rectangular rooms, etc. Compaction composition is very close, as a method, to *collage*, inasmuch as the superimposition of elements obscures parts, instead of allowing them to be seen through (except in the unique case of glass). Hence when one wanders through a Le Corbusier building one finds a succession of elements partly hidden and partly revealed. This accounts for their excitement and suspense. The monks of La Tourette [104], for instance, will conduct one through the building on a preferred path showing all the elements overlapping and changing relationship in a symphony of movement. This is most effective when the elements are pure in form and few in number.

One approaches Garches from the north down a driveway which focuses on the service entrance and balcony above [41]. The north and south façades are white planes, divided up by proportioned triangles on a 2-1-2-1-2 rhythm, which is also the column grid that disciplines the interior space. The feeling of an abstract rectangular order is further heightened by the blank side walls and the sequence of layered space on the south side, the garden entrance, which consists of a gigantic cube of space that is cut into from all sides by terraces, balconies, roof and wall planes [42-3]. This huge loggia recalls both the Italian villa and the ocean liner which Le Corbusier often used as sources [44]. The aesthetic of the building is finally determined by 'the five points of a new architecture': the free façade with its ribbon windows suspended from the floors, the free plan, and so on.

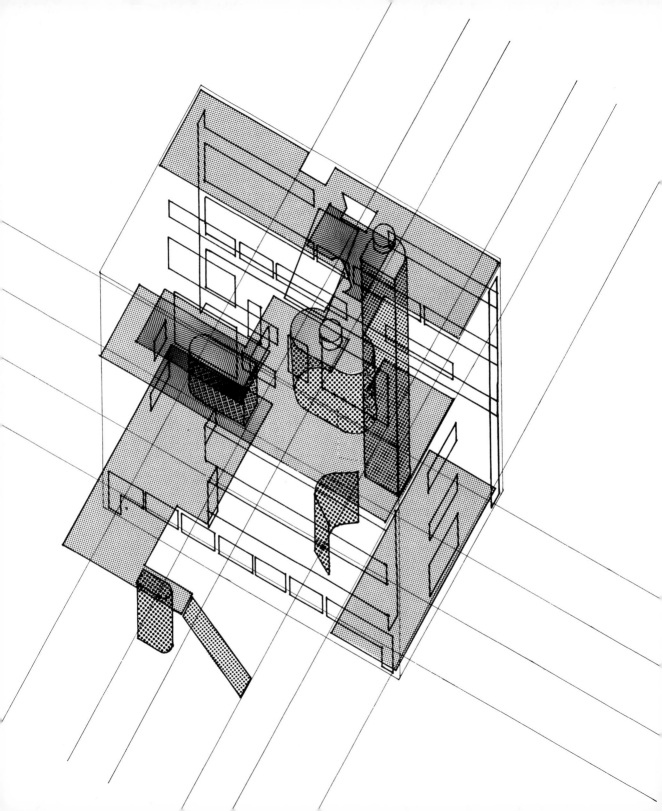

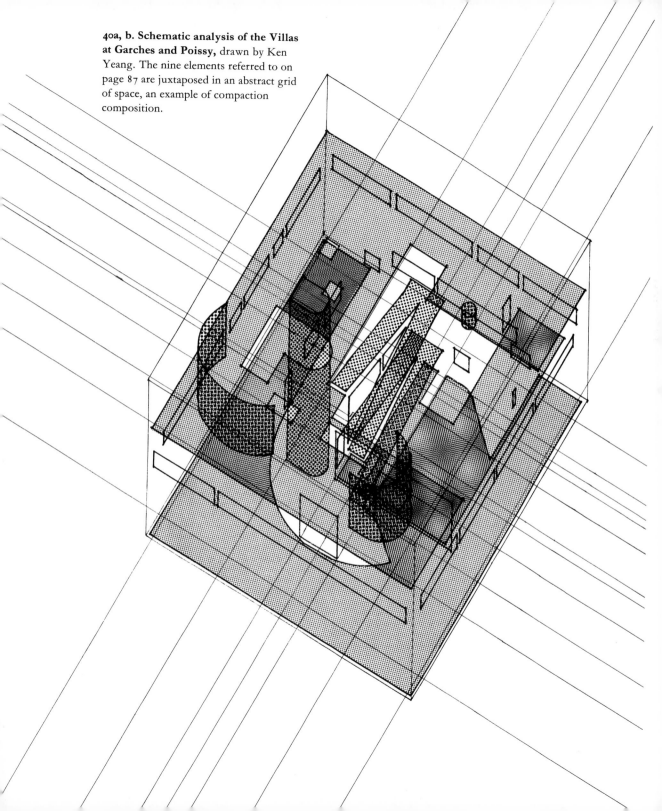

40a, b. Schematic analysis of the Villas at Garches and Poissy, drawn by Ken Yeang. The nine elements referred to on page 87 are juxtaposed in an abstract grid of space, an example of compaction composition.

(*far left*). **Villa Stein at Garches, 1927,**
north façade. A basic symmetry
punctuated by loggia entrance and black
openings. Le Corbusier's Voisin
automobile was often photographed with
his buildings to underline the nature of 'a
house like a car'.

–3 (*left and below left*). **Villa Stein,**
garden terrace and south elevation with
space flowing across white planes.

(*right*). **Illustration from**
Towards a New Architecture.

(*below right*). **Villa Stein, living**
room, 1929.

6 (*left*). **Villa Savoie at Poissy, 1929-31.**
<del>p</del>resent state. Classical echoes: a
<del>tr</del>ansformed, white entablature above a
<del>d</del>ark base in shadow.

<del>4</del>7a, b (*below left and right*). **Villa**
<del>S</del>avoie, entrance hall, and terrace.

Although Le Corbusier invariably photographed his buildings un-
furnished, to heighten the effect of pure forms in relationship, they still
provided a strong background even when filled with objects. This can
be seen by a rare photograph of the Garches villa when it was inhabited
by the Steins [45]. The photo shows that the Stein family had eclectic
taste, and yet the heterogeneous possessions do not seem overpowered
or out of place as they would in much modern architecture. Compaction
composition has provided a rich enough background to accept them
naturally.

The villa at Poissy is also a realization of the 'five points'. As well as
demonstrating these, it also has the characteristic elements such as the
entrance ramp (which cuts through the middle of the grid), the curving
walls of the solarium and, above all, the *pilotis* and slab construction. In

fact, for these last points it was attacked by architects such as Frank Lloyd Wright for being just a 'box on stilts' and others for being an alien space capsule that had just touched down on a Virgilian landscape [46]. It *is* a startling image, especially for the Paris region. A sharp pristine whiteness, a slab of brilliant ice, hovers gently over the ground, the very image of the '*machine à habiter*', a man made artefact in opposition to nature. The effect of a white cube poised above a flat green field is still startling today, even though the contrast has been partially destroyed by later building.

One approaches the villa by a driveway which circles around and under the first floor and between the *pilotis* in a curve which was functionally determined by the steering radius of a car. Once inside the ground floor, given over to services and servants, one can promenade through a sequence of primary forms and '*object-types*' either by a ramp, which penetrates up through the whole building, or a curving staircase [47]. The first floor, surrounded entirely by a ribbon window, consists of the complete living accommodation wrapped in an L on one side of the open terrace. Light and air penetrate everywhere. Direct contact with the surrounding landscape is achieved by various openings, views are framed like a picture. Verdure spills out of boxes on the terrace and solarium. The feeling of a heroic health camp is inescapable. The bathroom, with its tiled sunken bath and reclining sofa of tiles, reminds one of Roman gymnastics [48]. And it was the first demand of 'The Manual of the Dwelling':

'Demand a bathroom looking south, one of the largest rooms in the house or the flat, the old drawing room for instance. One wall to be entirely glazed, opening if possible onto a balcony for sun baths; the most up-to-date fittings with a shower-bath and gymnastic appliances.'[52]

Thus with these two buildings, Le Corbusier had brought to fruition many of the Purist notions and architectural principles he had been developing for at least ten years. They were immediately recognized around the world as the epitome of the new architecture and Le Corbusier was asked to give lectures in major capitals such as Moscow, São Paulo, Algiers, Stockholm, Barcelona, Brussels, and Prague. A new role was opening for him as the accepted polemicist for modern architecture. And yet, at the same time as these seemingly self-assured successes, doubts were developing which were to alter the nature of his approach.

At War with Reaction 1928-45

The change which Le Corbusier underwent between 1928–1945 was largely unconscious and has, for the most part, escaped notice. There was one explicit change in 1928, when he consciously introduced 'objects evoking a poetic reaction' into his paintings – i.e. substituted such things as shells, rocks and people for the Purist bottles, flasks and pipes. He was very deliberate about presenting this new approach to natural subject matter and biological form, as if it represented the noticeable aspect of a much more profound and hidden change. Perhaps the starkly programmatic statements are meant to be interpreted symbolically. At any rate four shifts were discernible: the turn to worldly pursuits, women, travel, lecture tours, friendship; the attempt to build a public realm on liberal institutions; a dominating interest in city planning, now based on curvilinear forms; and a deepened pessimism about the European cutural situation which was becoming both politically and artistically reactionary.

WORLDLY PURSUITS AND FRIENDSHIPS

In December 1930, Le Corbusier married Yvonne Gallis, an attractive fashion model born in Monaco. Ozenfant had introduced him to her in 1922. Le Corbusier's relationship with Yvonne, as indeed with other women, was never made a matter for public consumption, and the personal evidence which does exist consists in a few scattered remarks, various drawings, and the stories of friends and acquaintances – all of which does not amount to a very accurate or trustworthy account. Nevertheless a rough picture can be sketched which has a certain relevance to Le Corbusier's architecture and city planning.

Apparently, Le Corbusier lived with Yvonne for several years before pressure from his Swiss protestant family, not to mention from Yvonne herself, pushed him into a conventional, legal relationship that he might have wished to avoid. He was wary of taking on any personal responsibilities that would cut into his time and deflect his primary mission.

'When I was married, I said to my wife "no children" because I feared at that time that my life would be very hard as an architect.'[1]

Yvonne, from all accounts, was the kind of woman Le Corbusier was continually attracted to: not an intellectual, a good cook with an 'earthy' humour – interested in bawdy jokes and not at all in architecture – someone who could be counted on to break up solemn meetings of architectural luminaries, such as those of CIAM, by pointing out some hidden virtues of female anatomy. She had a sharp wit and, like Le Corbusier, loved to shock, even him. 'All this light is killing me, driving me crazy,' she said about the apartment Le Corbusier designed for her [49]. For her the aesthetic qualities of the glass curtain wall and the attempt to bring light into every nook and cranny of the house were folly, and she never really appreciated what her husband was achieving in architecture. Le Corbusier placed a bidet, that beautifully sculptural 'object-type', right next to their bed. She covered it with a tea cosy.

'A great event today: we brought upstairs, with great exertion, a large, homespun couch. All of a sudden everything took on an air of great comfort and calm, "like other people's houses". Yvonne was ravished. In addition, we could also serve ourselves coffee sitting on a sofa. It's like this one acquires by a long journey the rights to enter into bourgeois society.'[2]

The sarcasm, even cruelty, of such remarks was underscored by an Indian woman, Taya Zinkin, whom Le Corbusier tried to seduce once or twice, without success, in the fifties. As she tells it, the following unfortunate conversation took place.

'He spent the evening discussing women, prostitution, the importance of Indian males and his own wife. "I absolutely fail to understand her. Of course she is pretty stupid, *mais quand même!* I give her all the money she wants but that is not enough for her. No, Madame wants children! I *hate* children. She already has a little dog, that should be good enough. Take another dog, have two dogs by all means, but leave me alone is what I say to her. Children are the curse of society. They make noise, they are messy, they should be abolished.'[3]

As W. C. Fields said, 'Anyone who hates children can't be all bad.' One can doubt the import of these remarks (for instance Le Corbusier enjoyed the children of his friends, such as the Nivolas [85]) and the motive for Taya Zinkin's vicious portrayal (which will come out shortly), but still imagine that he said something like this in a fit of pique or as a heavily concealed joke. Le Corbusier's relation with Yvonne was not idyllic. Several French acquaintances have said that she was more than a woman of easy virtue; others have said she became an alcoholic and near cripple in later life and that Le Corbusier looked after her as a nurse. During the Second World War, she suffered from malnutrition, broke her leg as a result and lost much of her previous beauty.

The effects of all this must have been to isolate further a man who already had difficulty in close, personal relationships. Although Le Corbusier had many extremely devoted friends, he always remained an enigma to them and would not allow them to get too close. If they erred or betrayed him, *finis*. A characteristic action was his firing all the designers at 35 rue de Sèvres whenever they became tired, slack, old or uncreative. Once again he could burn what he loved, even if this was personal friendship. On the other hand, in certain respects he was utterly devoted to Yvonne, as he was to his mother. According to Walter Gropius, he suffered something of an extended breakdown when Yvonne died in 1957, and there are glimpses of a very strong and simple bond in a few photographs, paintings [50] and scattered remarks.

(*opposite*). **Yvonne Gallis in the ght-filled kitchen of their apartment,)34.** Le Corbusier captioned this photo: he kitchen has become one of the sential rooms in the house'. He saw the ousewife directing family affairs from a entral point and often gave the kitchen a rimary location and significance.

(*right*). **The painting by André auchant shows the two Jeannerets urting Yvonne, 1927.**

'Yvonne died yesterday morning at four o'clock, her hand in mine, in silence and complete serenity. I was with her at the clinic for eight hours, watching over her, she was the opposite of a suckling baby, leaving life with spasms and mutterings in a *tête à tête*, the whole of the long night. She finally died just before dawn. She was a highly spirited woman with a strong will, integrity and tidiness. Guardian angel of the home, my home, for thirty-six years. Liked by all, adored and loved by the simple and rich, the rich of heart only. She took the measure of people and things in that scale. Queen of a little fervent world. An example for many and yet without any pretence. For my "Poem to the Right Angle", she occupies the central place: character E3. She is on her bed in the guest room, stretched out, with her masque of magisterial and *Provençal* structure. During that calm day, I discovered that death is not a horror ... In gratitude to my wife for thirty-five years of wonderful devotion, for surrounding me with the blessings of quiet, affection and happiness.'[4]

These were the simple qualities which he enjoyed and if he was the mythical French husband whenever he travelled, at least he was faithful and considerate to Yvonne in Paris. Foreign female acquaintances who dared phone him at home received a standard answer: *'Connais pas'*, as he hung up.

The important aspect of Le Corbusier's relation to women and his friendships was the intense and even moral excitement they generated. This was recognized and underlined in the key words which he used to describe friends. A *'brave-type'* signified those such as Léger and Picasso who by creating beauty were actively doing good. *'Fidèle'* and *'sérieux'* were applied to reliable friends and pupils and to those who had the courage of their convictions. Le Corbusier found in Negro music, in the hot jazz of Louis Armstrong, 'implacable exactitude', 'mathematics, equilibrium on a tightrope' and all the masculine virtues of the machine. He describes a particularly moving encounter with the black singer Josephine Baker, whom he met while travelling to South America in 1929:

'In a stupid variety show, Josephine Baker sang "Baby" with such an intense and dramatic sensibility that I was moved to tears. There is in this American Negro music a lyrical "contemporary" mass so invincible that I could see the foundation of a new sentiment of music capable of being the expression of the new epoch and also capable of classifying its European origins as stone-age – just as has happened with the new architecture. A page turns. A new exploitation arises. Pure music. In the cabin of the ocean liner, Josephine grabbed a little guitar – a child's plaything – and she sang Negro songs. They were fantastically beautiful, touching, rich, inventive, generous and decent! ... "I am a little black bird who looks for a little white bird; I want a little nest to put us both together in," and "You are the wings of the angel who is come, you are the sails of my ship, I could not let you get away; you are the stitch of the cloth and I will place all of you into the cloth, roll it up and carry it around so that you can never get away from me" ... Josephine Baker, known around the world, is a small child pure, simple and limpid. She glides over the roughness of life. She has a good little heart. She is an admirable artist when she sings and out of this world when she dances.'[5]

The realistic portraits which Le Corbusier sketched of her singing and dancing brought out her simplicity and vitality.

One finds in the drawings of Josephine Baker and of other women an interest in the nude form which is part sexual and part sculptural [51].

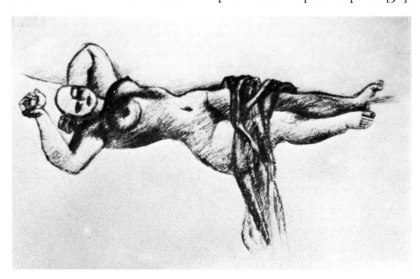

What starts off as fairly representational, the thighs, shoulders and bottom, ends up by the late thirties as stylized and distorted shape: rounded V-forms and broken ellipses. These are then incorporated into paintings and city planning [52]. If one looks hard enough at the plans

for such buildings as Ronchamp [88] and the Carpenter Center at Harvard, one can also find the curves of buttocks and shoulder arches. This is quite a turn-about for a man who had been damning the curve as 'the pack-donkey's way' and proclaiming that 'culture is an orthogonal state of mind'. No doubt a renewed contact with women changed his mind on that score. Most of the pencil sketches of the thirties are of elaborately distorted and heavy women. They are not pudgy or voluptuous like a Rubens, nor quite as calm and statuesque as Picasso's neoclassical nudes of the twenties, from which they may perhaps stem. Rather, they are gargantuan, muscular and peasant-like: the women of Algiers, athletic bathers, who are encompassed in strong flowing contours [53]. The priority of contour and profile over colour and shading remained from the Purist days even though the subject matter had changed from machinery to heavy women. Taya Zinkin was apparently the victim of this change.

'As we were getting off the plane he asked me what I was doing that evening: "Catching a train, I am afraid," I said. "Pity. You are fat and I like my women fat. We could have spent a pleasant night together." He said this quite casually. He was not being offensive, he was being factual . . . he took such a functional view of sex that it never occurred to him that the act would not carry its own reward for both of us . . . By the time he had had a few drinks he was paying me the sort of compliments Rubens must have paid to Hélène Fourmont when she was far gone with child. Had I not studied medicine I would have found his anatomical precision embarrassing. I had always known that I was fat, but I had not realized before that I looked as fat as all that.'[6]

The situation which Taya Zinkin describes was basically ambiguous from the start. She as a journalist was trying to get a good scoop from Le Corbusier – a fact which no doubt annoyed him as he was always disgruntled by journalists. The crude, functional and in the end unsuccessful seduction scene which she describes reflects as much on her own unsubtle tactics as on Le Corbusier's egoism, which she makes the part of her scoop. And while he did take a functional view of sex, just as he classified all human activities in an objective light, there are contrary stories showing a profound consideration for women. One of the more humorous accounts is given by Le Corbusier in *When the Cathedrals Were White*, a book written about his first trip to the United States in 1935 and subtitled, ominously, 'A Journey to the Country of Timid People'. The timidness was found in the architecture and sex of the Americans.

Sketch of two nudes, 1931.

A small section titled 'Everyone an Athlete' starts off with a positive view of the Vassar girl.

'I made a trip to Vassar, a college for girls from well-to-do families. From New York the car plunges north into Westchester; when the slums of New York have been left behind . . . we arrive at the college "within a budding grove" . . . a dozen girls are taking down the sets of a play put on the evening before . . . They are in overalls or in bathing suits. I enjoy looking at these beautiful bodies, made healthy and trim by physical training.

'The buildings have the atmosphere of luxurious clubs. The girls are in a convent for four years. A joyous convent.'[7]

Everything works out spectacularly well. Le Corbusier gives a talk, illustrated by drawings, to six hundred girls. After the lecture they swarm the platform, seize the drawings and rip them up for autographs.

'A piece for each Amazon. Pens in hand, they cry: "Sign, sign!" . . . The drawings at Vassar had a particular verve. The Amazons reduced them to confetti.'[8]

But afterwards another aspect of these beautiful athletes begins to emerge. A taste for the Mannerist painter Caravaggio.

'You women are also interested in Caravaggio? Why Caravaggio? Because of the psychological turmoil in that equivocal personality. Do you also feel a kind of frustration?" . . . Caravaggio, an Italian painter of the sixteenth century, "worked in a studio which was painted black; light came in only through a small overhead opening". Stop! Through him we discover a corner of the American soul. If we connect Caravaggio with contemporary surrealism which is well represented in American collections, our diagnosis will be confirmed . . .Caravaggio in university studies, surrealism in collections and museums, the inferiority complex which obsesses those who wish to break away from the simple arithmetic of numbers, the principle of family disturbances, the funereal spirit . . . [this] reveals, under well-bred external appearances, a complex disturbance and the anxieties of sexual life.'[9]

Thereafter follows a series of antitheses between Cubism and Surrealism, health and depravity, functional, cosmic love and fearful desire.

'The perpetuation of the species is a cosmic law; love, human creation, is the luminous joining together of sensuality and aesthetics . . . is it in the name of art, Vassar student, that you enter that sewer [of Caravaggio]? I believe that you were impelled by an unsatisfied heart.'[10]

Before continuing this account, we should note in passing that Le Corbusier had designed, four years earlier, a fantastic apartment for a collector of surrealist objects - really a surrealist apartment itself, designed with a Purist background[54, 55].Once again the rejection of a position is caused by its uncomfortable closeness, the way it almost but doesn't quite convince. Such is Le Corbusier's reaction to the 'Quat'z' Arts Ball' held in the Waldorf-Astoria Hotel in New York City - a continuation of his amateur psychoanalysis of the timid Americans. He contrasts again a healthy, creative nudity, the nudity of artists at the Quat'z' Arts cele-

Beistegui Salon, 1930-31. Electricity ...oves walls and even sliding hedges, ...t the room is entirely lit by reflected ...dlepower, candelabra skewered on ...rrors!

Beistegui roof garden with imitation ...ne furniture, grass carpet and daises. ...e position of the mirror accentuates ...rther the ambiguity between indoors and ...tdoors.

bration in Paris, with the self-conscious display and rented costumes of the ball in New York.

'As the painting is, so are the architecture, the decoration, the ball. The little nude women brighten up the affair, of course, and that is what makes it go. At the Waldorf-Astoria there will be no little nude women, oh, never!

'The costume man wants to rig me out with a turban and a brocaded robe; this evening, for the same amount of money, I can be a rajah or a khan.

'No usurped title, thank you! Not being a handsome fellow, I keep my anatomy out of sight. In spite of more protests, I insist on white and blue striped convict's trousers and an Indian army guard's vermilion coat (he would have loved to see me in a high-ranking officer's coat!); I find an enormous gold epaulette which I fasten on the left side. No military cap, sir, a white, pointed clown's hat, please, . . . to finish off, three differently shaped spots of white in my cheeks and forehead, to perplex the curious [56]. If everyone does likewise, there will perhaps be some amusing sights!'[11]

Needless to say everyone does otherwise, dresses according to the conventional rules of a costume ball, and the party is respectable, solemn and stiff. Le Corbusier is rejected.

'I was neither mad nor clownish, I was a sore thumb. I was out of place . . . Lost, poor fellow, I was the only one of my type, disagreeable, disapproved, rejected. I left ingloriously, thrust aside by respectability.'[12]

56. Le Corbusier, Josephine Baker and others at a costume party on board the *Julius Caesar, 1929.* Le Corbusier was forever dressing up as a clown or convict such parties.

The moral once again for Le Corbusier is the timidness of Americans, too insecure to create their own style, too conventional to invent their own fancy dress.

It is in this light that Le Corbusier's rejection of cosmopolitan life and urbane sophistication is relevant. He opens *La Ville Radieuse*, 1935, with the confession.

'. . . I am attracted to a natural order of things. I don't like parties and it is years since I set foot in one. And I have noticed that in my flight from city living I end up in places where society is in the process of organization. I look for primitive men, not for their barbarity but for their wisdom.'[13]

Out of this interest in primitive societies sprang a series of buildings constructed in a modern folk vernacular – what would be called the 'New Brutalism' twenty years later, because of the straightforward use of *béton brut*, raw concrete, and various coarse materials 'as found'. In the fifties, two of Le Corbusier's buildings, the Unité at Marseille and the Ronchamp Church, were interpreted almost universally as a dramatic rejection of the sleek, white machine aesthetic, but in retrospect it is now clear that Le Corbusier had already evolved his own form of Brutalism by the thirties. This is apparent in several projects and buildings constructed from primitive materials: the Errazuris house, 1930 [57], the house for the patroness of CIAM, Mme Hélène de Mandrot, 1931, the Weekend house [58], the house at Mathes, 1935, and finally the self-

(*below*). **Errazuris House, 1930, Chile.** The familiar planning elements such as the double-height living room and ramp are translated into a totally new aesthetic of rough timber and broken stone.

(*below right*). **Weekend House, 1935, Paris suburb.** The Brutalist aesthetic of exposed brick, raw concrete and industrial materials used 'as found'. As in many of Le Corbusier's houses the rooftop is submerged in wild grass which hides the volume.

built 'Murondins', 1940 [59], envisaged for the uprooted population of a Europe at war. All these houses make use of very simple materials ready to hand or found on the site: rough stone, fair-faced brick, raw concrete, unfinished timber, etc. And the intention is to create a very simple poetry from these materials: 'objects evoking a poetic reaction' or the definition of architecture made in 1923, 'the business of Architecture is to establish emotional relationships by means of brutal materials'. Hence one may conclude that by the mid thirties Le Corbusier had already made his move to Brutalism, a move that was prompted in the deepest sense by a rediscovery of natural orders, primitive societies and a sexual relation with women unconstrained by conventional etiquette, sophistication or snobbism. Several formal innovations in addition to Brutalism resulted from this change. Le Corbusier remarked to one of his designers in the atelier: 'The columns of a building should be like the strong curvaceous thighs of a woman' – and they were so designed in one or two cases [60], [79].

IDEAL LIBERAL INSTITUTIONS

While Le Corbusier was, in a sense, retreating from city life to the simplicity of the country he was, at the same time, becoming interested in the possibilities of a viable public realm. In the twenties, his city plans culminate ironically in an empty space in the centre: an airport, or business centre, that is a purely utilitarian institution. Partially this resulted from Le Corbusier's suspicion of the traditional church and state. Like so many modern architects, he had nothing but contempt for party politics and little respect for all the going political options, whether Capitalism, Communism, Fascism, Anarchism or National Socialism,

59 (*above*). 'Murondins', 1940-4. Self-built housing for refugees.

60 (*opposite*). **Swiss Pavilion, University City, Paris 1930-32.** Heavily modelled *pilotis* support the slab-block as 'legs' appropriate to their visual and anthropomorphic function.

etc. The only ideology which he could accept was that of his own construction, what might be called idealist liberalism. Like a true son of the Enlightenment he would accept only ideals as his guide, ideals based on reason. This allowed him, like Walter Gropius, to remain free from partisan involvements in a sort of apolitical politicism, sailing between the Scylla of Fascism and the Charybdis of Communism, a polarization which brought down most other architects in the thirties. Yet if this position had an intuitive, pragmatic brilliance, it also brought inevitable problems. All the clients had to be persuaded by idealist arguments (instead of party sentiments) and had to be enlightened paternalists on the order of Colbert or, at least, M. Fruges, the commissioner of Pessac.

Le Corbusier faced the ambiguity involved in this directly. He designed 'ideal workers' houses' in steel for the Ministry in charge of mass-producing houses. Five hundred thousand were to be built under an Act formulated by M. Loucheur. But just as Le Corbusier produced design after design, he would accompany them with the disclaimer, 'The right state of mind does not exist', 'There is no point of contact between the two sides involved: my plan (which is a way of life) and those for whom the law is made (the potential clients who have not been educated).'[14] In short, he would pursue enlightened and liberal ideals and then claim that the masses of people were incapable of living up to them. Thus he was led to the paternalistic idea that only a few great men were capable of initiating significant projects which would educate and transform the masses. He was supported in this idea by the emergence of several liberal institutions, such as the League of Nations, 1927, and the contact with utopian individualists, such as Paul Otlet, the client for the 'Mundaneum' and World City, 1929.

Both projects for the League of Nations and World City represented a form of internationalism popular to liberals after the First World War. These gigantic projects would contain respectively a rational world government and world culture, an assembly of all nations and a super-anthropology, a scientific collection of all customs, cities and tongues. In hindsight, it is perhaps a bit too easy to laugh at the naivety of the attempt. One has to imagine the idealism of the time, prior to the later failures of the United Nations, Unesco and other forms of internationalism. For Le Corbusier this internationalism was the basis for an emergent public realm.

The League of Nations [61] was laid out in many ways like a Renaissance palace with a series of perpendicular axes crossing a *cour d'honneur* which culminated in the *res publica*, the wedge-shaped Assembly Hall. A

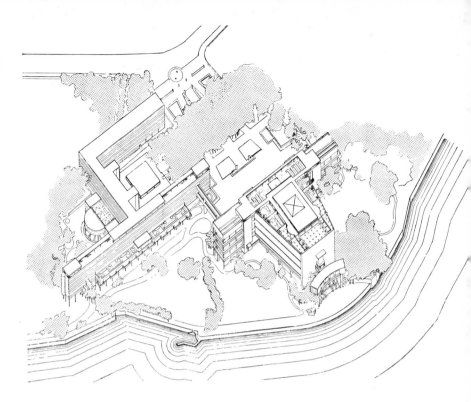

very clear hierarchy of elements is established, leading from the more utilitarian, the secretariat, to the symbolic, the agora or place of meeting. Not only does the Assembly Hall occupy the supreme position next to the Lake of Geneva, but its wedge shape and sculptural additions announce its priority over the rectilinear forms. A considerable amount of effort went into determining adequate sight and acoustic lines so that the 2,600 participants in world government could speak and be seen. In fact the wedge-form and parabolic section were innovations at the time which later became common to assembly halls, even their conventional and symbolic shape. But the project was excluded from a competition for the building on a technicality, because it was not presented in Indian ink. At the same time a small newspaper from the city next to La Chaux-de-Fonds started publishing a series of attacks on Le Corbusier by a Herr von Senger. These attacks were also instrumental in the failure of the project and they were later collected to be used by the Nazis to discredit modern architecture as well as Le Corbusier, who was featured in the title as *The Trojan Horse of Bolshevism*.

After this débâcle, Le Corbusier came back with another internationalist project to be situated right next to the League of Nations, the

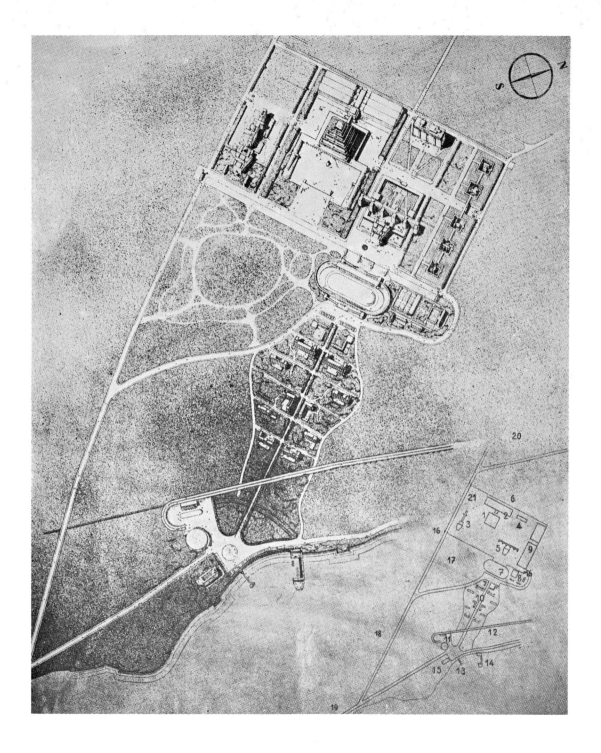

Mundaneum or the 'Centre of Centres' [**62**]. The programme for this was developed by a Belgian industrialist, Paul Otlet, baptized 'Saint Paul' by Le Corbusier for his efforts in spreading the message. In fact, the two prophets wasted a good deal of time and money giving lectures and putting on exhibitions trying to interest the Genevans in the World City. An extract from Otlet's manifesto gives an idea of their grandiose intentions.

'The goal of the Mundaneum is to expose and make known by literature, objects and words: How Men, from their humble origins, have elevated themselves to the splendour of their Geniuses, their Heroes and their Saints; – How the World was discovered and, its Forces being brought under control, was almost entirely settled; – How the Cities, Nations and Civilizations grew up . . .'[15]

For Le Corbusier the most exciting part of the project was the World Museum, a spiral in plan and stepped pyramid in section, which would show the various stages of civilization in continuous development. One would take an elevator to the top and middle of the pyramid (the beginning of civilization) and walk down in ever descending ramps until one reached the bottom (or the present day). A triple nave containing three kinds of information (the objects, where they were created and a description of the culture) classified man's knowledge in a typically French way. One is reminded of the Encyclopédie of the Enlightenment, or the French pursuit of Structuralism today, where the same synchronic and diachronic analyses are attempted. Yet the World Museum had two obvious faults. Being a hollow pyramid, it was terribly wasteful of interior space, and starting off with the beginning of man at the top, not only would it imply devolution rather than evolution to the present, but worse – have to burrow below the ground in the future! Thus in his next project for the Endless Museum, Le Corbusier flattened the spiral and allowed for unlimited, non-hierarchical growth. The idea of the World Museum was, in a sense, turned inside out and upside down by Frank Lloyd Wright and built as the stimulating Guggenheim Museum in New York. Le Corbusier himself constructed two Endless Museums, in Japan and India, none quite as spatially exciting as Wright's.

Late in 1929, Le Corbusier finally met an enlightened client who could realize one of his liberal ideals: providing healthy, even salubrious, habitation for refugees and the destitute. Mme la Princesse Singer-de-Polignac was instrumental in commissioning the Salvation Army Refuge in Paris and seeing this revolutionary building through to com-

pletion [63]. Like the previous two projects, this monumental building was a modern version of Beaux-Arts axial planning, with a series of elements disposed hierarchically in an architectural promenade. Because of the tight site, Le Corbusier was forced to push the elements together, laterally, in a very exciting way. A gigantic doorway leads next to a cantilevered canopy and thence to a curved entrance portico followed by a grand hall. The promenade culminates in the glass dormitory slab which contained two technical innovations: the 'neutralizing wall' and 'exact respiration'. Ideally, these inventions should have provided the inhabitants with pure, clean air at a constant temperature of 18° Centi-

63. Salvation Army, City of Refuge, Paris, 1929-33. The first glass curtain wall hermetically sealed with no window openings, but 'conditioned air' instead. Note Le Corbusier's car once again.

grade, but in the event, they were never completed for financial reasons and the refugees became rather uncomfortable in the summer. The 'neutralizing wall' was to be a form of double glazing with circulating hot and cold air between, while 'exact respiration' was to be a form of air-conditioning system, found in large buildings today, which supplies and extracts humidified air from a central system. Since the double glazing wasn't built, the dormitories overheated in the summer and openings and *brises soleil* were later provided, thus destroying the effect of the clear curtain wall.

Although Le Corbusier has been criticized by several people, such as Reyner Banham, for wishing to provide a constant environmental solution instead of flexible controls, it seems more to the point to com-

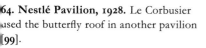

64. Nestlé Pavilion, 1928. Le Corbusier used the butterfly roof in another pavilion [99].

mend him for trying to innovate in an area where few other architects were trying. One of these, Pierre Chareau, was constructing *La Maison de Verre* in Paris at the same time – a building which made use of different types of glass and climate controls in a uniquely functional and poetic way. A strange figure with briar pipe, dark heavy-rimmed glasses and bowler hat was seen prowling the site early in the morning taking down notes and eyeing the glass brick. Le Corbusier was absorbing lessons not only from Chareau but also from the Russian Constructivists, and he produced at least two projects which owed a lot to them: the Nestlé pavilion of 1928 [64] which used blown-up graphics and chocolate

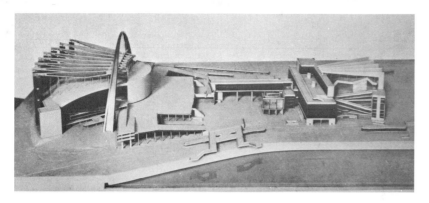

65a, b. Palace of Soviets, Moscow, project 1931. From left to right, the hall for 15,000 spectators, an open-air platform for 50,000, a long administration block, four halls at right angles, libraries and the main assembly for 6,500.

products to create a Constructivist collage of advertisement, and the Palace of the Soviets, 1931 [**65**], which outdid even the Constructivists at their own game of structural gymnastics. Two main assembly halls, both in wedge shape, are slung from giant, bony girders that cut across the sky like so many jagged saw-teeth. Below one the roof of the auditorium zig-zags back and forth following acoustic lines while above the other a parabola rises holding one half of the girders which in turn hold the auditorium roof. The dynamic clash of skeletal structures, dark glass and white volumes, all laid out on a symmetrical base, was appropriately equal to the grandiose nature of this Palace. The mania for gigantic spectacle which developed out of the Russian Revolution had found its architectural equivalent. Mass celebrations, the twenties version of today's pop festivals, find accommodation in a large, open-air platform.

Indeed the programme and lightweight steel architecture have an obvious parallel with what is being produced today by such designers as Archigram.

In spite of this brilliance, doubts remain about the nature of the functions envisaged. If the public realm depends upon being able to speak and act in public in such a way as both to disclose oneself and to intervene in political decisions, then the size of the assembly halls alone would condemn them to a certain irrelevance. They are at best containers of a mass society and its organized spectacles; at worst organs of a totalitarian state. In part Le Corbusier must have realized this because he spent a great deal of time detailing the lobby spaces, what he called the *forum*, where all sorts of quasi-political activities such as eating, talking and telephoning were accommodated [66]. In the event, the project was

66. **Palace of Soviets,** *forum* under the assembly for 15,000. Le Corbusier finally built such a grand space of columns and walls in the General Assembly at Chandigarh [91e].

rejected by a jury because it looked too much like a factory and, more important, because Stalin had decreed that proletarian architecture must be Greco-Latin in spirit. The Palace of the Soviets was to built in the Italian Renaissance style, and just as the people had taken control of the banks away from the bourgeoisie, they would also appropriate their Corinthian columns. So the Stalinist argument went. Le Corbusier's attitude towards this débâcle was not his usual fury. He actually justified the decision to build in the Renaissance style as understandable in view of the youth of Russian revolutionary culture. Only a civilization in maturity, at its high point, could have accepted the severe lyricism and technical brilliance of his solution. In fact, Le Corbusier's grand cultural theories were clouding the issue. The rejection and reaction was due to nothing more nor less than Stalinism, a point which many other Western intellectuals also

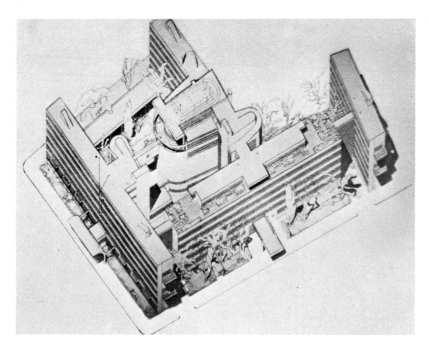

67. Centrosoyus, first project 1929.
A basketball court crowns the central
assembly, the public realm.

didn't understand for a long time, partly because of wishful thinking,
partly from ignorance. The only building that Le Corbusier managed to
get built in Russia, the Centrosoyus, 1929–33 [**67**], was a caricature of his
intentions and the public realm – a monolithic office block gross in scale
and without the intended air-conditioning system. It wasn't really until
the fifties and Chandigarh that he had the opportunity to build the public
realm on such liberal institutions as he imagined and worked for in the
thirties.

PARTICIPATION AND THE RADIANT CITY

During the thirties and until the end of the Second World War, Le
Corbusier devoted a great deal more time to city planning, perhaps
because he received few architectural commissions and hence had the
time to undertake theoretical studies. His output of city plans is remarkable, not only in sheer size, but also in terms of futility. Few were
commissioned, fewer still were paid for and perhaps none stood the
slightest chance of being adopted. This may account for the new tone
which is descernible in Le Corbusier's writings: diffuse, repetitious,
sometimes bombastic and always now in an extreme hurry. Books are

120

thrown together so fast from collected articles that their author has to apologize for mistakenly publishing an article twice. But –

'In the very first pages of this book I have warned you that this not a work of serenity, written in the calm study of a man of letters.

'Alas! that serenity is not for us!'[16]

The tone becomes hysterical and, unfortunately, infectious. Many books on city planning, some written by CIAM members, sound like the millennium is at hand and, as a result, all sorts of liberties are taken with the reader which wouldn't be tolerated in a time of peace. The city planner is at war with a society which will not listen to him, whether he screams or talks sensibly. What are the new themes which emerge from this period of incessant turmoil? First of all the necessity for active participation which is preached in *La Ville Radieuse* and *When the Cathedrals Were White*, both of 1935.

'Rome meant enterprise. They invented Roman cement. The Republic, *res publica*, was the object of all their care. The public good was the reason for the city and also for their arrival in the city. Participation in it was their life.'[17]

If Le Corbusier is here idealizing the Roman public realm (participation was more a reality under the Greeks) he positively goes overboard about the Age of Faith.

'When the cathedrals were white, participation was unanimous, in everything. There were no pontificating coteries; the people, the country went ahead. The theatre was in the cathedrals, set up on improvised stages in the middle of the nave; they told off the priests and the powerful: the people were grown up and masters of themselves, in the white church – inside and out. "The house of the people", where they discussed mysteries, morality, religion, civil affairs, or intrigue was entirely white . . . we must get that image into our hearts.'[18]

The political method for inducing this participation, pointed out at the beginning of this book, was to be a form of anarcho-syndicalism, where workers' unions would form the basic power structure and send representatives to a federal centre [1]. Le Corbusier found two current examples of participation in action and they are exceedingly odd given the previous models of the forum and medieval commune.

'The Van Nelle tobacco factory in Rotterdam, a creation of the modern age, has removed all the former connotation of despair from that word "proletarian". And this deflection of the egotistic property instinct towards a feeling for collective action leads to a most happy result: the phenomenon of *personal participation* in every stage of the human enterprise . . . The Managers, the highest and lowest grades, the workers, male and female, all eat together here in the same great room, which has transparent walls opening onto endless views of meadows. Together, all together . . . Participation! I can truly say that my visit to that factory was one of the most beautiful days of my life.'[19]

If this modern factory of steel and glass designed by the Dutch Constructivist Mart Stam was a current version of the white cathedral, so too was the Ford motor factory in Detroit.

68. Algiers Viaduct building, Plan Obus, 1932. A curvilinear roadway on top of dwellings made by the inhabitants in different styles including Moorish, Louis XVI, Italian Renaissance and Modern. Compare with photo [52].

'In the Ford factory, everything is collaboration, unity of views, unity of purpose, a perfect convergence of the totality of gestures and ideas. With us, in building, there is nothing but contradictions, hostilities, dispersions, divergence of views, affirmation of opposed purposes, pawing the ground.'[20]

What is odd here is that Le Corbusier can so easily confuse a unified communal effort like harmonious factory-work with political participation, or the necessary plurality of views in the public realm. It was this confusion of the smooth-running factory with the good state that made him rather easy on Fascism. In architectural terms his idea of participation leads to the viaduct building, the artificial building site where every individual can build his own villa in whatever way or style he wants [68]. This involved public ownership of the artificial sites, but a complete freedom within that limitation. The idea has become very popular today with certain theorists such as Nicolas Habraken and might find present application where self-built environments are a possibility, such as the *barriadas* of Peru. It makes a great deal of economic as well as social sense to separate the public support system from the private dwelling and let the individual have full control over the latter. Here participation can result in a much richer and more responsive environment. What is surprising, given Le Corbusier's great interest in participation, workers' unions, the public realm and such liberal institutions as the League of Nations, is that none of this is adequately translated into the city plans. There is no forum or public realm, beyond a few cultural institutes; the business centre still occupies the symbolic and functional place of importance. Perhaps this is because Le Corbusier still equated the Captains of Industry with the state's leaders, or Ford Motor Company with a public realm. In any case what he continues to do is divide the city up into four functions – living, working, circulating, recreating – leaving out the political and public function until much later in the 1940s. His general scheme for the Radiant City develops on the biological analogy with the business centre as the head, housing and institutes as the spine, factories, warehouses and heavy industry as the belly [69]. The biological analogy leads of course to the separation of functions, or 'organs'. Le Corbusier makes this his keynote.

'A plan arranges *organs* in order, thus creating *organism* or *organisms*. BIOLOGY! The great new word in architecture and planning.'[21]

And the biological analogy extends so deeply into the forms of city planning that when Le Corbusier is flying over the rolling landscape of

123

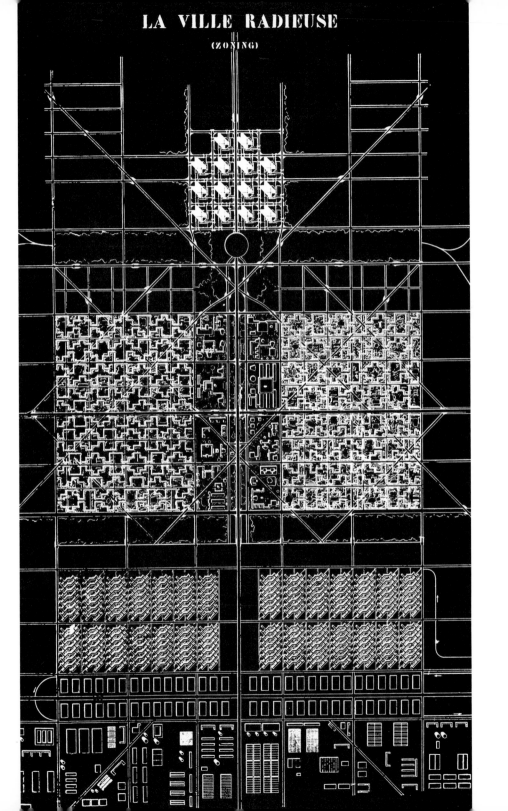

LA VILLE RADIEUSE
(ZONING)

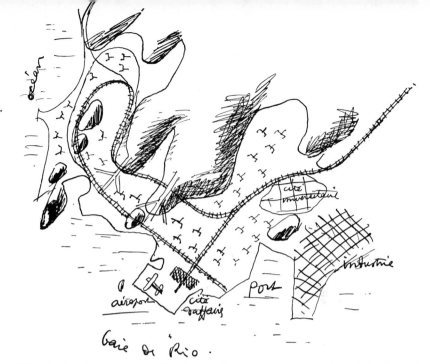

Rio de Janeiro he can suddenly see the topography as a female body and introduce curvilinear forms into his city planning [70].

The thing that sparked off this link between his interest in women and city organization was the aeroplane, in praise of which he wrote a book in 1935. The aeroplane with its bird's-eye view reveals a new truth about cities and discloses principles of organization which have previously remained hidden, just as the microscope has done. The aeroplane thus has the same mixture of implacable truth and lyricism that Le Corbusier admired in science books and statistics. It allowed him to get, literally, above the normal anthropomorphic view and reclassify the accepted urban categories. These became 'The Three Human Establishments'. For the dispersed suburban sprawl, which he saw from the areoplane, he substituted the cooperative 'Radiant Farm', for the strip developments along routes, he substituted the 'Linear Industrial City' and for the sprawling city itself, the 'Radio-Concentric City of Exchange' [71]. All of

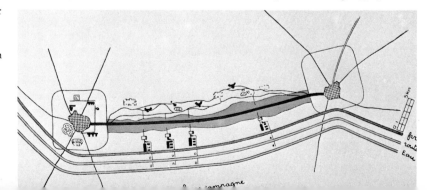

this was quite a departure from his previous ideas which were against dispersal and very much against concentric rings of city growth. One may attribute this change to the realities which were seen from the plane.

In the idea for the Radiant Farm, Le Corbusier projects an image which has a very touching mixture of peasant life and industrialization [72].

The farm is mechanized and prefabricated, but the simple, everyday objects of the farmhand are given an exaggerated importance. Perhaps most important of all is the idea of the Cooperative Centre which distributes communal machinery to the farmers and sells their products as well as providing a new element of village life, the communal club. In this proposal one gets the rare glimpse of Le Corbusier's regional-syndicalism and participation actually resulting in a city plan.

72. **The Radiant Farmhouse, 1935.** Herculean peasants listen to a radio cantilevered from an I-beam. Silos and animal sheds are in the background.

REACTION AND COUNTER-ATTACK

Throughout the thirties and early forties there was a worldwide reaction against the modern movement which was directed against its leaders, for example Walter Gropius, Le Corbusier and Leonidov, and its various avant-garde organizations, such as the Ring, CIAM and OSA (the Association of Modern Architects in Russia, 1925–32). Le Corbusier, as the best known and most articulate of these leaders, took the brunt of the attack and was, in the event, the only one to mount any sort of counter-attack. The other leaders did not write books against reaction; they went underground, into exile, or collaborated with the mounting nationalist movements. Walter Gropius wrote compromising letters to Rosenburg and Goebbels, Mies van der Rohe signed anti-semitic manifestoes and worked for the Nazis until 1937, Moholy-Nagy fled Germany.[22] In Russia the Constructivist architects mostly just stopped working and were not heard from any more. In Italy, Fascism compromised virtually all of the modern architects by adopting a style of stripped-classicism and commissioning such rationalist designers as Pier Luigi Nervi and Giuseppe Terragni. In America a similar kind of stripped-classicism combined with Hollywood Art Deco became the ruling style of design. Everywhere a pompous, semi-historicist architecture reigned supreme. To live through this period as a modern architect was like living through Diocletian's persecutions as an early Christian – a question of compromise and sometimes bare survival. Le Corbusier's record during this period is, like that of so many others, full of ambiguities. It started with the nationalist attacks on his work and the loss of many commissions, such as the League of Nations competition.

'M. de Senger published his second book [in 1931]: "The Trojan Horse of Bolshevism". The horse, that's me. The newspapers of Neuchâtel and La Chaux-de-Fonds continued to dredge up this source of clear water and republished these decisive articles. One day, I received from my city of birth, La Chaux-de-Fonds, three editorial articles from its newspaper, consecrated to my collusion with the Soviets, my spurning my country and the beauty of art. My father honorary president of the Swiss Alpine Club, my mother the musician, had left in La Chaux-de-Fonds a memory filled with great dignity. The life of my great-aunt, who was for me another mother, was full of devotion, charity, love of God and noble works. The day I received these articles, I cried with the knowledge that she would read such abominations . . .

'What stuff for newspaper writers of great and small papers! written to be copied. And modern architecture born about 1830 in Paris, became Bolshevist in Geneva, Fascist in the Paris "Humanité" and petty-bourgeois in Moscow (where gable and column have again come into style), recognized only by Mussolini [see his speech to the young architects in June 1934]. A match is of course a small and unimpressive thing, and yet, it may be the beginning of a catastrophe. This campaign of Senger was not without success: two years later the "Figaro" in Paris began a series of articles from the talented pen of Camille Mauclair with a sharpness bordering on the ridiculous. These attacks were based on the "heroic" articles that appeared in 1927 in the "heroic" "La Suisse Liberale" of Neuchâtel. The great "Figaro" succeeded in discovering this hero and fulfilled its noble mission of saving Fatherland, Beauty and Art and whatever else was wanted . . . "Is Architecture going to die?" This was the title of the book of Camille Mauclair. He certainly needs to be consoled: "Camille you have lost your head, console yourself, Architecture is far from dying, it enjoys the best of health . . . it only demands that you leave it alone!" '23

The arguments that Senger, Mauclair and the Nazis used against Le Corbusier were the following. First, architecture should be an embodiment of national glory, territoriality and such specific determinants as race, climate and local materials. The international modern architecture was supposedly none of this, although Le Corbusier answered that it was (in such things as the Eiffel Tower which embodied French aspirations).24 Second, flat roofs and ribbon windows were ugly and unpopular, being defended only by international Marxists and the bourgeois press. Le Corbusier countered this by saying that Moscow was now in favour of capitals, Corinthian columns and pitched roofs. Third, L'Esprit Nouveau and CIAM were pro-Bolshevik, Jewish conspiracies which were trying to convert people to a modern style in order to convert them to international Communism. Le Corbusier answered this by saying that L'Esprit Nouveau published critical articles on Lenin, that CIAM contained Gentiles as well as Jews and that the new architecture was apolitical in any case. Finally, Senger took two of Le Corbusier's aphorisms literally, as did many more liberal critics, and accused him of inhumanity. 'The machine for living in' would destroy the family and territoriality and the statement 'man is a geometrical animal' was untrue. Le Corbusier countered these remarks, perhaps understandable distortions of his own overstatements, by saying that a machine is meant to aid not dominate us and that the work of man, his constructions and perceptions, are geometric in nature. These counterattacks were contained in a book written by Maximilien Gauthier and published in Paris during the war. In fact many of the arguments were so degraded that it was obviously compromising even to answer them in any detail, and thus imply that they had some plausibility. But Le Corbusier, unlike the other modern architects, was never above polemics or what amounted to architectural street-fighting. He fought the world-wide reaction in a series of pamphlets, books and buildings.

Crusade – or the Twilight of the Academies was published in 1933 to answer Senger and a certain Professor Umbdenstock of the École des Beaux-Arts, who had launched a campaign against Le Corbusier. Here the academies had combined with nationalism and the traditional building trades to condemn modern architecture because it was supplanting the older forms of building and putting many craftsmen out of work. This economic attack was naturally financed by many of the building trades, and, actually, capitalists. It further confirmed Le Corbusier's suspicion of all moneyed interests whether they were capitalist or socialist. *Crusade*, like *When the Cathedrals Were White*, was a sort of mock religious tract. It contained the usual aphorisms and prose-poems followed by a series of alternating photos comparing, unfavourably, the academic conceits of Professor Umbdenstock with either healthy sporting events or the beauty of machine instruments. The lecture was the professor's original attack given at the École in 1932 and it is actually printed in part at the end of *Crusade* (without the professor's permission). Le Corbusier makes the most of Umbdenstock's attack by writing witty answers to each point in the margins – an extension of his tactics as a manifesto writer and fighter.

Because of this aggressive stance against moneyed interests and the establishment, the Communist party of France tried to enlist Le Corbusier in the Popular Front against Fascism. The Civil War in Spain, National Socialism in Germany, and the friendship of Communists such as Fernand Léger and Paul Vaillant-Couturier almost persuaded Le Corbusier to join the Popular Front. But in the event all he did was go to their meeting and design a monument for Vaillant-Couturier who died in 1937 [73]. Characteristically he turned a political platform into a building programme.

'From my point of view, there exists only one way for the Popular Front to demonstrate that something new has begun on the scene of social justice: that would be to construct right now in Paris the elements for habitation which reflect at the same time the latest state of modern technics and your wish to put such things in the service of men.'[25]

The monument reflects very aptly the qualities of fighting against social injustice which Le Corbusier found in Vaillant-Couturier. It makes use

of conventional motifs present in French art of social protest, the screaming mouth and jutting hand which Delacroix and Picasso also used symbolically.

However, as for Le Corbusier's actual commitment against Fascism, it was, to say the least, fitful.

'In Rome, 1934, my two lectures were authorized after two years of argument by the youth of Rome and the Academy, by an intervention of Mussolini which took place at the beginning of the second lecture: the public reading of a message affirming the necessity of modern ideas concerning architecture. This was in answer to a vote of the Senate, fifteen days previously, declaring modern architecture antifascist. It was by the decree "nulla osta" that Mussolini had authorized my presence in Rome for these two lectures before the unions, on the architectural and urbanistic revolution. He summoned me to an audience, but, as he happened to be then with Hitler in Venice, I returned to Paris . . .'[26]

Another story has it that Le Corbusier took his plans for the Radiant City to Mussolini saying, 'You've made the new state, here's the new architecture and town planning to go with it.' Obviously Le Corbusier held to a certain type of *cultural* élitism which could be compromised, or at least confused, by the political élitism of Fascism. In one diagram he actually puts forward the idea of a cultural pyramid with the avant-garde élite at the top, the romantic and academic group in the middle and the poor 'good people', confused and misdirected, at the bottom.[27] This pyramid was no more than a description of taste as he found it – led by a small aristocracy – but it suggests how being too realistic might lead to being too reactionary.

All Le Corbusier did in a reactionary sense was go to the Vichy government in 1941, try to work for them for a year, and write two books at this time with his quasi-Fascist friends Dr Pierre Winter and François de Pierrefeu. Of course this *was* collaboration and enough to condemn him in many people's eyes, particularly other modern architects who went into the Resistance. But the collaboration occurred in 1941, when things were still rather ambiguous, and in a way which revealed Le Corbusier's peculiar inability to compromise on a single point in which he believed. He worked for the Pétain government not to construct monumental edifices, but rather self-built houses for the uprooted refugees. A commission more at variance with this régime could not be imagined and it was laughed out of court. One of the things to confuse Le Corbusier was an act of the Vichy government made at the end of 1940 which allowed only three architects without official diplomas to practise: Auguste Perret, Eugène Fressynet and himself. Hence it appeared that Vichy was supporting three of the most uncompromising modernists: Vichy in fact put Le Corbusier and Perret on a committee for reconstruction.

'The minister Peyrouton, who had just arrested Laval, proposed that I go defend my ideas in front of my own *confrères*. I accepted, I went to Vichy, but they refused my entry on the commission. By chance I met, through a common friend, a member of the state council in charge of making building laws. The opportunity was present for the first time in my life, being always rejected by administration and thereby deprived of official data, to be able to know the general data at the national level and thus the power to think of urbanism on a scale hitherto inaccessible for me. The twenty-seventh of May 1941, a decree signed by Marshall Pétain gave me a temporary mandate for the creation of a State organization, the Committee for Housing and Real Estate. With François de Pierrefeu and André Boll we attempted to define a doctrine of the built environment for France. I thought I could at last carry out the proposals of the preparatory committee of urbanism previously worked out with Jean Giraudoux in 1939, but a débâcle cut everything short. The director in charge of *equipment general* said: "neither close – nor far – nor under any circumstance, will I work with Le Corbusier and Pierrefeu . . . " '[28]

74. Algiers skyscraper project, 1939–42.
The lozenge-shape. *brises-soleil* and
complex articulation make this vertical
city as comprehensible as the horizontal.
A restaurant and hotel at the top, offices
behind the *brises-soleil* and archives in the
three solid bands.

Le Corbusier was sent by Vichy in 1942 to carry out some planning proposals for Algiers – among other things his skyscraper project which remains to this day one of the most radical solutions [74]. But his presence wasn't welcomed either by the CIAM architects, who were embarrassed by his connections with Pétain, or by the local government, which was concerned about his alleged communism – Senger's book having just reached Algiers. The Mayor of Algiers let it be known that he would arrest Le Corbusier as a Bolshevik agent. Quickly Le Corbusier returned to France, and he spent the remaining years of the war in extreme destitution, painting and organizing plans for a future reconstruction. His one collaboration with state officials ended in disaster which he expressed with characteristic bitterness.

'*Town planning expresses the life of an era.*
'*Architecture reveals its spirit.*
'Some men have original ideas and are kicked in the arse for their pains.'[29]

Le Corbusier was really trapped with his brand of apolitical politics in a vicious polarization between the Communists and Vichy. There was no room for a man who would collaborate with an authoritarian government in order to set up libertarian reforms. For his part, Le Corbusier understood this fact and hence reversed the normal forms of etiquette in an act which was as humorous as it was arrogant. When the Communist Party asked him to join them during the war, 'I told them it was they who ought to join me.'[30] This inversion of customary practice would explain his collaboration with Vichy. It was done not for personal gain nor opportunistic reasons, but rather to realize certain ideals which were held to be independent of politics. Hence his collaboration was different from that of Gropius or Mies van der Rohe because it did not involve the compromising of architectural ideals. His architecture, unlike the others', remained as tough, sharp and brilliant as ever. One may deplore his ideals and actions at this time, and the naïvety of his thinking that Vichy would allow libertarian schemes, but one cannot doubt his integrity and the complete honesty on the level at which he was committed in his deepest being: architectural. Perhaps the artist, who has by definition to go beyond everyday experience, is allowed limited political failings, a lack of *realpolitik*, which other citizens are not allowed, as Hannah Arendt has argued in an essay on Bertold Brecht.[31] What the artist is not allowed is the compromising of his art for political motives. This Le Corbusier never did.

Other Languages of Architecture 1946-65

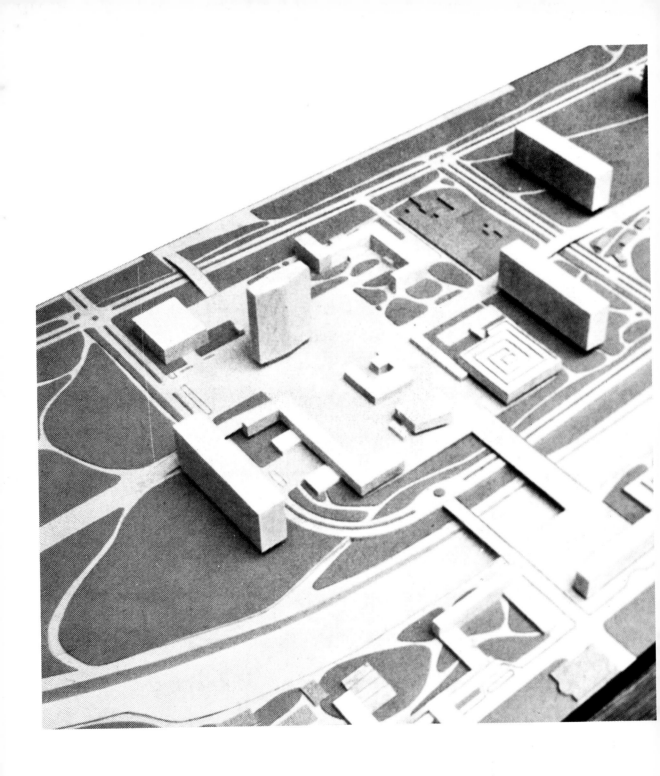

After the Second World War, Le Corbusier took up the challenge of reconstruction with a vigour and spirit that were comparable to his efforts after the First World War. He developed a new aesthetic, tough and realistic, towards the poverty of reconstruction, and set the major task confronting architecture as rehousing the uprooted masses – four million families in the case of France. In this burst of creative strength he was virtually alone. The other established modern architects, many of whom had settled in the United States, were content to carry through their pre-war ideas and settle into successful practice. The International Style became officially accepted everywhere and, in a watered-down and sterile form, the style for vast schemes of reconstruction. Hence the popular reaction against modern architecture which occurred in the fifties and sixties. In retrospect, the surprising thing about this post-war period is that it did not generate the excitement and liberation which the end of the previous war had done. There were no new movements akin to Expressionism, Purism, Dada, and Constructivism. Perhaps the exhaustion of war and the pessimism it seemed to imply as a chronic and inevitable state had a dampening effect on men's creative capacities. Destroyed cities were built up on the outlines and styles of the past. The undestroyed sewer systems often served as an argument for keeping to the old road patterns and building plots. Le Corbusier, almost alone, protested against the lost opportunities and offered, once again, a 'new spirit of the age' appropriate to the situation, as he saw it. In this case, the spirit he proffered through his buildings and paintings was primitive, more realistic towards the aggressive aspects of man, and explicitly sensual. If the war had undermined his faith in the machine civilization, it liberated a new belief in formal gratification. In a word, Le Corbusier conceived architecture as sculpture in a new plastic language.

THE BRUTALIST LANGUAGE

Le Corbusier's first and most influential plan for reconstruction was for the bombed-out city of Saint-Dié in Eastern France. In this scheme he put forward his first real crystallization of the public realm [75]. Unlike his previous city plans, the civic centre and market-place – the agora – occupy the primary space. This space is conceived as a vast pedestrian precinct which would allow the citizens to perambulate around their civic monuments and meet on an informal level in cafés and shops. The value of this informal meeting Le Corbusier understands as necessary to the formation of opinion, of political points of view.

Saint-Dié plan 1945. A vast, open piazza containing isolated buildings which can be seen from all sides. The piazza is dominated by a government tower, the pie-shaped communal halls and an L-shaped block of cafés and shops. An industrial green belt is to the south and residential 'unités' to the north.

'A French apéritif is taken when you are seated around a table. There are two, three, four persons. You have chosen your companions. You drink slowly. Conversation is calm, interrupted by the silences of well-being: you talk, you discuss, you can even enter into disputes. But the idea is followed through. Thus personal ideas are born, points of view, opinions. It is an agora around a siphon. The apéritif is a social institution and the café terrace is an urban institution.'[1]

In formal terms, the influence of the Saint-Dié plan has been very great, resulting in such urban projects as the Boston Government Center with its vast, pedestrian precinct and free-standing monuments of different scale and shape. Unfortunately these projects do not contain Le Corbusier's small-scale shops and outdoor cafés and thus tend to become windswept plazas devoid of people. As for the Saint-Dié plan itself, it was rejected by all sides of the political spectrum – the industrialists, socialists and communists – in favour of an academic reconstruction along the lines of the old city. While this rejection was occurring in

76 (*below left*). **Loggia of Unité d'Habitation, Marseille, 1947-52.** Each apartment has two heavy balconies which have a direct view of nature.

77 (*below*). **Unité, East Façade.** Complex articulation, heavyweight push-pull, the three-dimensional façade – all radical departures of post-war architecture were seen here for the first time.

1946, Le Corbusier was under way on two more projects which were also to have a great effect on post-war architecture: the United Nations building in New York City and the Unité d'Habitation in Marseille.

The Unité, or Marseillian Block as it is sometimes known, represents the culmination of Le Corbusier's research into housing and communal living. It synthesizes ideas going back to his travels of 1907, particularly the relationship between the individual and collective which he admired in the monasteries of Ema and Mount Athos.[2] Like these monasteries, the Unité provides total individual privacy, something like a monk's cell for each member of the family, and meaningful collective activities – actually twenty-six different social functions – varying from a gymnasium to a shopping centre on the seventh and eighth floors. Thus the inhabitants, who have formed a collective association, are bound together like a small village (of 1,600 people) in shared, everyday life, yet no individuality is sacrificed as in a small town or monastery because each apartment is acoustically separated and in direct contact with the surrounding mountains and seascape [76]. The feeling of protection and individuality is so strong that it is comparable to standing in a cave. Yet the overall feeling is not cave-like or even monastic but more of being on a gigantic ocean liner ploughing through the choppy seas of verdure and haphazard suburban sprawl [77]. The sheer physical presence of this ship-like monolith is overwhelming. Its power and weight are crushing. Its sculptural boldness and aggressive outline are so emphatic that, although it is now

8. Unité, 'The roof and a landscape worthy of Homer'. Each element is full blown and given an emphatic gesture.

actually smaller than some surrounding buildings, it still radiates a presence throughout the landscape. These visual meanings, comparable to those of the Acropolis, were quite intentional on Le Corbusier's part, especially on the roof [78] which he speaks about with the same metaphors he found in the Parthenon in 1911:

'The spirit of power triumphs. The herald, so terribly lucid, draws to the lips a brazen trumpet and proffers a strident blast . . .

'The sentiment of an extra human fatality seizes you. The Parthenon, terrible machine, pulverizes and dominates . . .'[3]

The Unité is in every way as keen, sharp and terrifying as the Parthenon. In fact the same effects are achieved by the same means. A straightforward functional simplicity exaggerated in its plastic effect and – what is not often seen in metaphorical terms – the power of proportion. The whole building is constructed from fifteen basic dimensions, 'Modulor' dimensions, which are related to each other in simple, harmonic proportions. These relationships give a semantic strength quite apart from their numerical ratios and it may well be that the Modulor (Le Corbusier's system of proportion worked out at this time) will be valued for this rather than its particular dimensions. For what it brings to a building is the *fullness*, even dignity, of each constructional element. They are all allowed a plenitude of space and gesture. None is cramped, or hesitant or truncated as in so much architecture where one part obscures or denies another. Rather, by giving each part its ratio to another, a relationship is set up between them which implies a humane, mature and dignified discourse among equals. Why is this dignity found in so much classical architecture and not in other kinds? Perhaps because the adoption of a proportional system itself leads to particular visual meanings: harmony, restraint, a set of dramatic relationships where no single part is allowed unduly to usurp the presence of the whole. One thinks of the pyramids of Egypt or the Pantheon in Rome or the villas of Palladio which achieve certain feelings of grandeur and one concludes that perhaps the semantic meanings of all proportional systems are the same regardless of their favoured ratios and dimensions. Yet while an overall harmony is common to these buildings, individual meanings vary greatly.

Thus the Unité is seen, metaphorically, not only as a ship and monastery, but by the critic Peter Blake 'as graceful as Joe Louis on tiptoe'.[4] Indeed there is the graceful power of this heavyweight boxer in the taut 'legs' of the building [79] and the violent push-pull of elements – heavy

a. Unité, the anthropomorphic nature
the south elevation.

volumes punch up into the sky and the sides are so many staccato jabs. Perhaps the emergence of this three-dimensional architecture actually owes something to Le Corbusier's image of himself as a boxer [2]. At any rate, a tough anthropomorphism is evident throughout, even in the 'Modulor Man' who is incised in concrete by the entrance, with legs apart and a gigantic fist raised above his head. At the inauguration of the building, Le Corbusier used an anthropomorphic metaphor to justify the crude aesthetic, the *béton brut*, the raw concrete, which was to become the insignia of the New Brutalism and post-war architecture.

'The defects shout at one from all parts of the structure! Luckily we have no money! . . . Exposed concrete shows the least incidents of the shuttering, the joints of the planks, the fibres and knots of the wood, etc. . . . in men and women do you not see the wrinkles and the birth marks, the crooked noses, the innumerable peculiarities? . . . Faults are human; they are ourselves, our daily lives. What matters is to go further, to live, to be intense, to aim high, and to be loyal!'[5] [80]

79b. Unité, anthropomorphic elements such as legs and spine carry the air-conditioning, sewerage, rainwater, plumbing and other utilities – all with open access between the concrete 'skin'.

. Unité, exposed shuttering and pre-
st concrete elements with exposed
bble aggregate – two aesthetic qualities
hich Le Corbusier discovered by
cessity. The Unité was initially conceived
steel, which proved too expensive
mediately after the war.

'Loyal concrete', a material Le Corbusier invested with all sorts of human qualities including even 'dignity and truth'. The interesting aspect of this is that he is also prepared to see it as crude and ugly and therefore as a possible means of contrast.

'. . . I have decided to make beauty by contrast. I will find its complement and establish a play between crudity and finesse, between the dull and the intense, between precision and accident. I will make people think and reflect, this is the reason for the violent, clamorous, triumphant polychromy of the façades.'[6] [81]

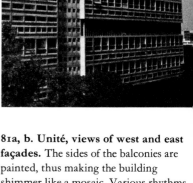

These façades are in a sense the antithesis of those of the twenties. Instead of being an ideal, flat plane, where even the glass line and the façade are on the same level with no projections such as a cornice, or mullion, or drip-moulding, these façades are violently sculptural in their depths and protrusions. Intense rhythms flow over the surface. Light and dark rectangles alternate at a certain tempo and then are inverted or played at twice the speed. This is the most musical of Le Corbusier's buildings and perhaps the one of which he was most proud. He spent a day with Picasso going through the building very carefully and mentions with obvious satisfaction that Picasso thereafter wanted to come into his *atelier* 'to see how one makes architectural plans'.[7] In one sense, Le Corbusier valued this artist's opinion above all others, as he considered himself the Picasso of architecture, and both of them as the equals of

81a, b. Unité, views of west and east façades. The sides of the balconies are painted, thus making the building shimmer like a mosaic. Various rhythms are played at different rates: architectural polyphony.

Phidias and Michelangelo. Yet his other commitment was to the social plane and it is here that the Unité made a great contribution, although one that has been heavily criticized.

The Unité is a 'temple to family life', to private and domestic life centring around the mother and the daily meal. Each family apartment (there are twenty-three types) has the kitchen as its centre, from which the mother can direct domestic affairs [82]. The children's bedrooms are placed furthest from the parents', thereby allowing a certain psychological and acoustic privacy. Unfortunately, the children's bedrooms are

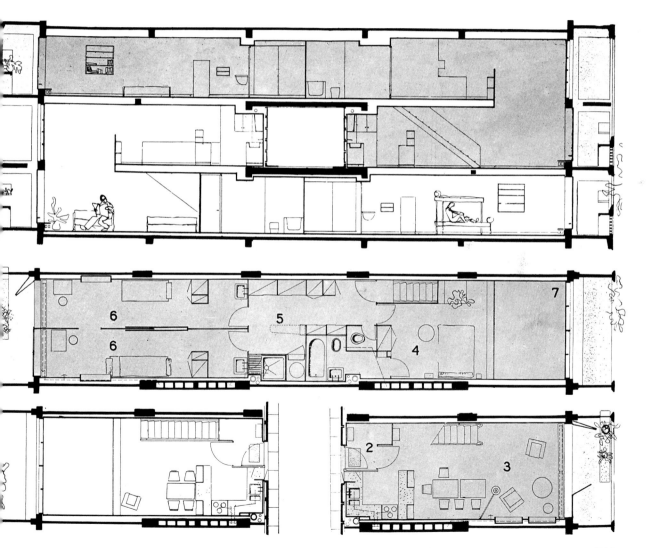

82. Unité, interlocking section. Interior streets run through on every third floor. The parents' bedroom looks out over the double-height living room.

145

little more than six feet wide (unless the partition wall is slid back) and they are more like railroad cars or bowling alleys than places to sleep. Nevertheless, the strong Mediterranean sun lightens their deep interiors and the exterior loggia provides a feeling of greater space. The life inside the apartments varies a great deal and is not at all homogeneous or standardized as many critics have stated. In fact there is the kind of personal transformation of abstract structures which one finds in Pessac and Garches. Postcards on sale at the Unité show a 'bar salon' placed in the children's bedroom [83]. The image is a wishing-well or gazebo

83 (*left*). Unité, 'bar-salon', with partition wall slid back.
84 (*opposite*). Unité, shopping street containing fish, meat, fruit and vegetable stores as well as a bakery, liquor and drugstore. A post office, hotel and restaurant are located near by. The photograph shows the quieter end of the street with architects' offices and coiffeurs, etc.

located in the garden and while this image may appear kitsch or improbable, it shows the popular transformation which is actually quite prevalent at the Unité. Why should people personalize this architecture where they might not dare change so much other modern work – that of Mies van der Rohe for instance? Is it because of the crudity and informal detailing? Television aerials and washing decorate the balconies. The walls of every apartment I saw were filled with bric-à-brac [76]. Perhaps this is provocative architecture which asks to be modified and territorialized. In any case, it provides a strong frame for variable urban living which is not destroyed when it is taken over and personalized. In providing twenty-three different apartment types, Le Corbusier went much further towards the pluralism of urban life than his detractors would like to admit.

The same is true of the shopping centre which has received much, to my mind misguided, criticism [84]. Located half-way up the building on the seventh and eighth floors, it has always been faulted for being cut off from the ground, from the connection with the external life of the street. Hence its supposed lack of life and financial viability. Shops remained unrented and the centre empty for a long time. But this was due, as much as anything, to the maladministration of the centre where the state demanded that shops be bought and not rented – too high a risk for a small proprietor to take. Today all the spaces have been sold and the shopping street really is a marvellous alternative to the hustle and bustle of the market place that one can find everywhere else in Marseille. It is very much like the commercial centres on an ocean liner: a calm, urbane space, very close at hand, which the housewife can run to in her curlers and slippers without feeling ill at ease. To think that it should be the only form of shopping would be an obvious mistake, but it does give the inhabitants of the Unité a choice, where other comparable developments have none, and a very strong feeling of communal identity. This is further enhanced by the great amount of collective facilities, such as the gymnasium, which bring small groups together around a common activity. One can find children playing on the roof, wading in the pool, not just when supervised by their mothers or the nursery attendant, but at any time – because the roof is quiet and safe, unlike the urban street. All in all, the Unité is what it was intended to be – a radical alternative to suburban sprawl, where groups of 1,600 people form a manageably-sized association that gives the benefits of individual privacy and collective participation in one unity. If this unity lacks one element, it is the public realm and political space that are implied in an autonomous unit of this nature and which can be found in its utopian predecessors of the nineteenth century. It seems strange that, given the ship, monastery and *phalanstère* as obvious influences, Le Corbusier has not provided a place for the captain or general assembly. An odd, perhaps unconscious, reason for this might have been the continuing series of disastrous political events in which he was involved at the time.

The Unité was designed and built under nasty pressure. 'Five years of storm, spite and uproar . . . dispicable, ugly. A hue and cry by the press.'[8] Ten changes of government, seven successive Ministers of Reconstruction. A suit was brought against Le Corbusier for disfiguring the French landscape. Doctors claimed that the Unité would produce lunatics. Meanwhile, Le Corbusier was having his United Nations project taken over and watered down by the American architect Wallace Harrison. His role in designing the UNESCO building in Paris was vetoed by the Americans the day before they made him an Honorary Member of the National Institute of Arts and Letters. Every contact with the actual world of politics had ended in defeat and bitterness. Why have a public realm, if politics was as petty and nasty as this?

While Le Corbusier was in the States battling over the United Nations scheme, he spent a lot of his time in retreat from the world, staying with his friends the Nivolas in the countryside of Long Island. There he relaxed into an almost domestic tranquillity, played with the Nivolas' children [85], took long walks on the beach and worked on a new form of sculpture developed by Tino Nivola [86]. This consisted in working directly with natural forces and rhythms: waiting until low tide and then working like mad to form the wet sand into a mould, covering it with quick-drying plaster and then removing the sculpture before the

85 (*above*). With Pietro Nivola, 1950.
86. Sand cast, painted sculpture, 1951.

148

tide had come in again. The results of this 'action sculpture' had to be crude and respectful of the simple possibilities of the medium: but clearly conceived, continuous forms could be achieved. They resembled the action painting of Jackson Pollock who was also working in Long Island at the time – although Le Corbusier felt this artist and the New York School would be judged, ultimately, second-rate. 'Pollock is a hunter who shoots without aiming.'[9]

This last remark typified Le Corbusier's distrust of the solely intuitive approach and it should be seen as indicating his preference for a rational, complex approach to art. Hence his programmatic statements on regulating lines, the function of murals and 'ineffable space'. He brought these three preoccupations together in a mural covering two walls of the Nivolas' living-room [87]. The function of a mural was, as he saw it, to create space in cramped areas and break up closed, rectilinear surfaces. 'Good walls' were to remain white. The Nivolas' mural does,

87. **Mural in the Nivolas' living room, Long Island, 1951.** From left to right: two interlocked women, a thick wall section in zig-zag pattern, a false door and biomorphic forms from the 'Ubu' series. These last forms were incorporated into Ronchamp [88].

in a sense, break down the protruding cube on which it is painted. This is due partially to the large, flat areas of contrasting colours which suggest a layered space and also to the strong curving profiles which contrast with the rectilinear walls and floor. The subject matter itself, surrealistic in content, also opens up the space: a false door is painted opposite a real opening, giving for a second, the illusion that one could walk right through the wall. The quality of 'ineffable space' which Le Corbusier was developing both in his painting and architecture can also be found in the mural. In part what he means by this term is the inter-relationship of formal elements, their setting up a series of tensions within a proportioned area so that each form can develop fully in relation to the whole. More than other painters of the twentieth century, Le Corbusier composes his paintings so that space can flow evenly through and around forms. They are never cramped. But also 'ineffable space' means the action of the forms on the surroundings, the way they radiate outwards and 'take possession of space . . . vibrations, cries or shouts (such as originate from the Parthenon), arrows darting away like rays, as if springing from an explosion'.[10] This idea of ineffable space was fully developed and realized in the chapel at Ronchamp in eastern France.

This pilgrimage church is situated in a rolling landscape and its white shape against the green hills can be seen from miles around. Its sculptural

88 (left). **Ronchamp Chapel, 1950–55,** from the east, the outdoor assembly area with the functional elements conceived as gigantic sculpture: the altar, pulpit, chapel hoods, stairway, etc.

89 (opposite). **Ronchamp,** south wall. Light wedges are cut into thick wall allowing diffused light to reflect on the sides. A thin wedge of light separates the wall and dark ceiling.

forms take in the four horizons, sometimes protruding out into space, sometimes embracing it [88]. The interior and exterior spaces also form a kind of counterpoint with the roof sloping downwards, the wall sloping outwards and the floor away from the roof [89]. All the forms respond to each other, send out a call which is answered. The building is almost plastically over-related. Take away one sculptural element and another will fall flat; exaggerate one too much and another will disappear. The kind of antiphonal balance is so exact that one can call it a rationally perfected piece of sculpture. Actually it was widely interpreted as a highly irrational building, a retreat from the modern movement, and a primitive piece of technology built of sludge (i.e. sprayed concrete) instead of the crisp, rectilinear, lightweight steel which modernism seemed to be all about. The architect James Stirling and the critic Nikolaus Pevsner, as well as countless others, were highly disturbed by what they took to be an expressionist building.[11] Indeed within the politics of the modern movement, Ronchamp probably did act as the catalyst for a neo-expressionism, precisely because it was interpreted as such. Yet there was nothing really new in the curvilinear forms, as far as Le Corbusier's work was concerned, and they were in fact all rationally determined. Besides their plastic interrelationship, they are all variants on the straight line and right angle. That is to say, Le Corbusier has taken a rectangular grid, proportioned by the Modulor, and distorted

it in various directions as if it were a piece of india-rubber. The remnants of this underlying grid can be found everywhere: in the floor lines and wall rectangles, etc. [89].

Perhaps a reason that so many modernists found this building disquieting is its elusive metaphorical quality. All sorts of images seem to be suggested – a nun's cowl, a monk's hood, a ship's prow, praying hands [90] – and denied at the same time. It is as if some specific mystical interpretation existed for every form while the language which would unlock their secrets had been lost. The anxiety of the critics can be compared to that of archaeologists who have discovered a beautifully articulated text they know to be nonsense. Because the forms are plastically exact, they appear to be determined by years of religious ritual and iconography. Yet Le Corbusier, the atheist and non-conformist, specifically rejected all conventional, religious motifs and approached the problem psychologically.

'The requirements of religion have had little effect on the design, the form was an answer to a psychophysiology of the feelings.'[12]

or, as he expressed it more emphatically still –

'[Journalists at Ronchamp] virtually machine-gunned me with their flash cameras. I told the workmen near me: "If these people don't get

90. Ronchamp, south wall, with apparently random fenestration: 'Swiss cheese' façade or 'cotton candy'?

out of here immediately take them by the shoulders and . . ." One of these fellows who had pursued me in front of the altar of pilgrimage outside, called to me, "Mister Le Corbusier, in the name of the manager of the Chicago Tribune, answer this question: was it necessary to be a Catholic to build this chapel?" I replied, *"Foutez-moi le camp!"* '[13]

In spite of these outbursts and denials, Ronchamp has been interpreted by many as the most religiously convincing building of the twentieth century. Partly this must be due to Le Corbusier's religious attitude towards cosmic truth and natural law which, although atheistic, was in every way as serious and profound as the attitudes of conventional religion. Yet it is also due to his powers of imaginative integrity. Like a plausible fiction of the writer Borges, Le Corbusier has constructed an alternative world that is as tantalizingly rich and believable as the real one, having all the coherence one expects except conventional reference. He may call this fiction 'ineffable space' or 'visual acoustics', as he does in describing Ronchamp, but it is as much 'plastic integrity', or imagining new forms and then resolving their interrelationship until they seem necessary and inevitable.

Le Corbusier's work at Chandigarh in the fifties represents the culmination of this plastic integrity as well as his new, heavyweight aesthetic. However, at Chandigarh there are some obvious formal as well as

1a. General Assembly, Chandigarh, 1953–61, from the 'picture window' of the Secretariat.

functional mistakes. The capital complex, created to the north outside the city, is too dispersed, both for the officials to walk from one building to another and to appreciate the juxtaposition of monuments – except

as distant vistas [91]. The intention was to create an acropolis of monuments which would radiate out its presence for miles, even to the distant Himalayas, and while this intention may have been realized, it has resulted in an over-monotonous fixation on each monument, unlike the Athenian acropolis where the buildings are much more intensely related and can thus be experienced together.

Within the monuments, however, relationships are so intense as to make what I have termed compaction composition even more compacted. In the General Assembly, the two main legislative halls are suspended in a grid of triple height space while they also slam through

91b, c, d, e. **General Assembly and Secretariat, Chandigarh, 1953-61.** The main assembly hall is under the hyperboli shell with its symbols of the sun and the council chamber is under the pyramid. A tilted concrete portico masks the entrance, *brises-soleil* indicate offices and flat concrete signifies the stairways.

154

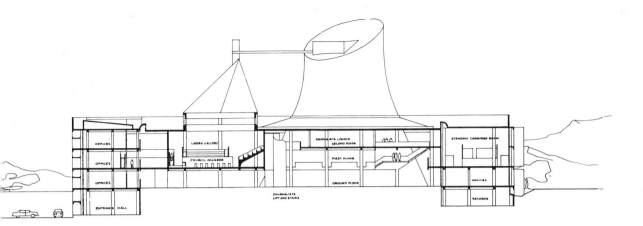

the horizontal roof line as a hyperbola and pyramid. The repetitive *brise-soleil* is stopped by a flat expanse of concrete and punctured by a horizontal walkway. Within the building, columns, ramps, lifts and lighting troughs interpenetrate in a way which is Piranesian and can only be described as violent. Yet because the Modulor was used to harmonize the relationships between forms and because there is plenty of free space within which to suspend these forms, none is truncated or compromised.

In fact this open space is devoted to what Le Corbusier once again called the Forum, that informal place of conversation and rest where delegates can pause and formulate opinion between meetings. This is virtually the only public realm that he was lucky enough to build. It has a dignity which is appropriate, yet its freedom from convention keeps it from being pompous. Within the main hall of parliament, Le Corbusier has also followed the democratic notion of the forum without falling into conventional notions of an hierarchical organization. He has abolished the speaker's platform, the place where programmes are announced, not debated, in the usual pseudo-democratic assemblies and instead provided each 'orator' with his own microphone so that he can be heard equally and interrupt the course of political events. This practice of participation was envisioned even for the people as well as their representatives. A 'Trench of Consideration' with a monument to the 'Open Hand' was planned for the capital complex, a place where ordinary citizens could debate public affairs. Unfortunately this open-air place has not been built and the subsequent political history of East Punjab has made it an unlikely building for the future. The other monumental buildings at Chandigarh are less successful than the General

92a, b. Courts of Justice, Chandigarh, 1956. Nine high courts are protected by rhythmical *brises-soleil* and a gigantic parasol which keeps out the sun and rain and allows air to circulate over the courts.

Assembly. The High Courts [92], although noble in outline and dynamic in detail, have suffered a series of alterations due to lack of functional foresight. A concrete sunshade had to be added at ground level because the courts were overheating. Not enough courts were provided, nor a system of easy expansion, so that when additional courts were built, they had to be suppressed, visually and functionally, at the back of the building. The eminent judges themselves started to disfigure the architecture by parking their cars under the gigantic, three-pillared entrance. They didn't like to park with the rest of the people, especially those under judgement. Finally, the judges switched the operation of the courts around, placing themselves against the brilliant light. How could you tell if the accused were lying if you could never see his face because of the glare? These functional shortcomings were typical of much of Le Corbusier's work at Chandigarh. They show, perhaps, both his greater age (he was now in his middle sixties), and the fact that he spent much time in Paris while work was still going on at Chandigarh. He delegated much of this work to his old collaborator Pierre Jeanneret, who undoubtedly deserves credit wherever the workmanship shows a high quality in spite of the primitive technologies. That Pierre Jeanneret could carry through such a visual masterpiece as the Secretariat Building while the designer was absent brings up the question of Le Corbusier's particular method of design and invention, a method which allowed a certain amount of interpretation and execution by others.

THE REPERTOIRE OF INVENTED SIGNS

Almost every architect keeps a file of his favourite details. Usually these consist of products on the market or else conventional modes of practice; a prefabricated staircase or a method of joining concrete and glass. The reasons for this filing cabinet approach are obviously economic but also aesthetic. It doesn't pay to reinvent every detail from scratch any more than it is enjoyable to manipulate completely unfamiliar material. Just as one speaks with ready-made words, the architect builds with pre-existing elements and in both cases, language and architecture, this traditional repertoire actually allows tradition to be extended and invention to be possible. The linguist Noam Chomsky has recently stressed that with fixed language rules and finite grammar, one is allowed, indeed made able, to generate an infinite number of new sentences.[14] In a like manner, the architect's creativity is somewhat dependent on his using a pre-existing syntax (or structure and technology) and semantics (or the conventional connotations of doors, windows, stairways, etc.). The difference between language and architecture is a matter of degree. The architect can much more easily proffer new elements than an individual can coin, and have accepted, new words. And the architect can change the relation between form and content much more easily than the speaker can alter the conventional associations between sound and sense. In these ways architecture is more flexible, permissive and changing than language, but at the same time less powerful for manipulating ideas and communicating. We will continue to speak words rather than buildings in spite of Saul Steinberg's cartoons.

The relevance of this linguistic analogy to Le Corbusier is that he regarded it as the architect's duty to create a new language.

'It seemed to me that I was at the end of the road of logic. I had touched at the essential principle: The architect dispenses new words – we will see!'[15]

We have already seen how he tried, with partial success, to create three new languages: a naturalistic, geometric Art Nouveau at eighteen, Purism at thirty-one and Brutalism at fifty-nine.

Like so many rationalist architects before him, Viollet-le-Duc and August Choisy, Le Corbusier conceived these new languages to stem directly from a change in technology. Given a new material such as steel, a new syntax and semantic naturally follow. Hence his most programmatic statement on the 'Five Points of a New Architecture' – those five new building elements which result, naturally, from the perspicacious use of reinforced concrete.[16] This rigid technological determinism would be of limited relevance were it not coupled with a broader interest in all aspects of formal invention whether they stemmed from the past and his travel sketchbooks, or the present and biological drawings. For this inclusive approach allowed him to invent a repertoire of new forms, or architectural signs, which were both technically based and semantically rich. He could build up an original stockpile of such signs which could handle a functionally complex problem. In a sense, he could design a whole city using just the words he either invented or else perfected. In fact his later city plans are filled with these 'words' – the endless museum, the pie-shaped assembly, the Unité, the *brise-soleil*, etc. [77]. It is worth pausing a moment over the method he used to create them.

Essentially, he would start with the rationalist method, as formulated by the eighteenth-century French functionalist Abbé Laugier, from which he often quoted.

'It is necessary to start at zero. It is necessary to state the problem . . . "If the problem is well stated, the solution will be indicated." '[17]

In creating a new word for his architectural vocabulary, the *'ondula-tories'*, which he first used on the Secretariat at Chandigarh [93], he restated the 'problem of the window' as four separate functions: to air, to ventilate, to view from, and to let in light. The four functions which are somewhat compromised in the traditional sash window are pulled apart and each satisfied by a new form. The various *brises soleil* shade the glass wall from the sun; vertical, pivoting ventilators of sheet metal allow fresh air in – otherwise ventilation is achieved by fans; finally the fixed glass wall, obscured at points for indirect light and open

3a, b. Secretariat, Chandigarh, 1958.
Almost eight hundred feet long, this
must be one of the longest bureaucracies
in the world. Various Corbusian 'words'
break up the mass such as the double-
height spaces, the loggia, ramp volume and
roof garden.

at other points for view, answers the two last 'problems of the window'.
The system of *'ondulatoires'* taken as a whole then constitutes a new word
in Le Corbusier's vocabulary to be used on the next building. This
method accounts for the freshness and distinctiveness of all his work.
A building by Le Corbusier can always be recognized as his own, even
though many of his words have become architectural clichés. Perhaps
the reason for this clear identity is the emphasis placed on each element.
The loggia stands clear from the wall [76], the ramp is separated by

colour and indentation [31], the roof is sometimes lifted clear off the rest of the building [98]. Loggia, ramp, suspended roof – none of these architectural words are radically new in the sense that mechanical air-conditioning was new in 1900. Their innovation consists in being seminal expressions of pre-existing elements, or final plastic solutions to functional problems. Because they have this visual strength and because they are also functionally based, they have been taken over and re-used by a much larger variety of builders than a singly determined form would be. They have become the morphemes of modern architecture, or units of architectural meaning. The forms of Ronchamp have appeared on banks in Los Angeles and *brises soleil* have appeared even on the north elevations of solid façades! Both these transpositions of intended usage show the arbitrary nature of the architectural sign.

An architectural element can always be used in a new functional context for which it was not intended. Formalist architects such as Philip Johnson have always been delighted by this permissive aspect, claiming, from time to time, that 'form follows previous form, not function'. In fact the relation between form and function is much more complex that either the formalists or functionalists would allow and if any generalization can be made, it would be the rather obvious one that there is a cybernetic relation between the two aspects, or that they continually interact in a dialectical way. To prove this, the example of the functionally based porcelain toilet is often cited. If it is transposed to an alien culture where the more natural forms of relieving oneself are still in practice, it is often used in new ways – to wash grapes or bath in. No doubt given time and semantic explanations, the toilet would finally become used as intended, until it achieved, as in our culture, its final culmination as a beautiful object in art history. Its sculptural properties would be explored. Still, in spite of these extensions in its use, this white, enamelled object would have a definite, partly fixed meaning in the culture which was determined by its initial function. A toilet is a toilet, but also more than a toilet.

The relevance of these considerations for Le Corbusier's architectural language is that it shows the same mixture of partial stability and freedom. He invents a new usage, such as the inclined building for protecting a stadium, and then finds new functions for this shape when it is moved across the site [94]. Or he is impressed by the hyperbolic shapes of industrial cooling towers and transposes this shape to the entirely different function of a church or general assembly [91]. There is enough of this transposition in all his work to disprove for ever the charge that

he was a straightforward functionalist.[18] And yet many of his architectural words remain functionally stable: the *brise-soleil* for example. This coherence of use allows one, when well enough acquainted with his work, to read off the semantic meaning of the architecture much as past ages could decipher their own classical language of architecture. The systematic deciphering and classification of Le Corbusier's archi-

94a, b, c. Youth and Cultural Centre, Firminy, designed 1956; built 1963–6. This inclined linear building was initially meant to shield a stadium on one side. Although the functions and placement changed, the inclined shapes remained and suggested a third form, the suspended, catenary ceiling. This balanced formula, two outward canting walls plus a hung ceiling, was then taken up as a unit of architectural meaning around the world, resulting in such buildings as Saarinen's Dulles airport and Alphonse Reidy's Museum of Modern Art, São Paolo, Brazil.

tecture has yet to be done, but it is obviously possible because of the stable and coherent use of form. It would be possible to analyse the basic units of meaning. Some of these, like the 'Five Points of a New Architecture', Le Corbusier has already partially analysed, and I have found another thirty-five (ramps, *ondulatoires*, etc.) which he was less systematic about presenting.[19] These forty points could be classified according to their function and semantic weight, until one understood the coherent usage. Finally, one could read off the specific architectural messages in each building, and find what attitudes and values were being communicated. Partially of course this would just confirm the multiple interpretations which the work had already received, but it would also give more precision to the actual plenitude of values which he presented. It would reveal, perhaps, the fullest world a modern architect has developed, a plurality of meanings which could encompass, or at least mirror, the complexity of modern, urban life. Like Frank Lloyd Wright or Picasso, this plenitude of values, this *embarras des richesses*, rests on a creative potency that seems almost inhuman, an act of nature rather than man. At least forty new words and two new aesthetics which changed the architectural language twice. There were also hints of yet another contribution to architectural vocabulary.

A LIGHTWEIGHT, RESPONSIVE LANGUAGE

While Le Corbusier was primarily attracted to the pure forms of a volumetric architecture, a white Mediterranean architecture made in different forms of masonry, he was also attracted to the machine aesthetic, an architecture of steel and glass, an architecture which might take its cue from ocean liners, aeroplanes, automobiles and the Eiffel Tower. This latter preference, always a minor theme in his work, might have become the major preoccupation had he built in a time and place where steel was plentiful and conventionally acceptable in architecture. He designed mass-producible steel housing several times, but with the realization that it wouldn't be accepted because 'the right spirit doesn't exist'. The only examples of glass and steel housing which he actually got built were two apartment blocks, one in Paris, 1934, the other in Geneva, 1931, which were really just tentative essays in the new aesthetic; rather dry, monotonous, and sterile, like so much functionalist work of the thirties. Yet in three exhibition buildings later on, Le Corbusier showed what wit and lyricism could be attained with a lightweight technology. Had these three buildings been accepted with the same acclaim as his heavyweight creations, we might have arrived at the mobile, responsive architecture of the sixties much earlier. They contain that interest in audio-visual techniques combined with flexibility that has become so strong today.

The 'Pavilion of New Times' was built in 1937 as a short-term exhibition to propagandize the 'lyricism of modern life' and educate the people in the new science of urbanism [95]. As such, the content as

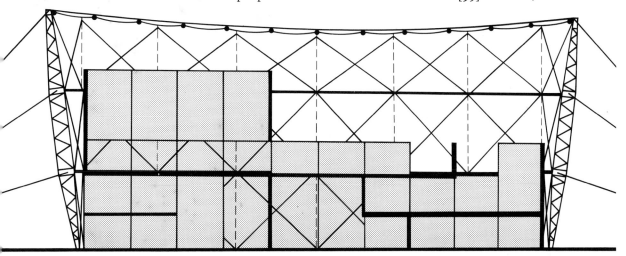

well as the form of this exhibition tent were very much of Le Corbusier's own choosing. One followed a clear path of circulation which had a didactic message that unfolded in time. The first set of images, a collage of words, photos and drawings, proclaimed 'the revolution in architecture is accomplished'. From there one went on to the CIAM analysis of urbanism, the four urban functions, various city plans, the Radiant Farm and finally to the exit – 'the understanding of the true programme for a machine civilization'. All of this had a heavy, dogmatic tone as the sections indicate. Yet some of the images were extraordinarily light and dynamic and became, in a sense, a greater reality than the ephemeral structure which enclosed them.

This shift in emphasis from form to content or medium to message became stronger in Le Corbusier's next exhibition tent constructed for Philips at the Brussels World Fair in 1958 [96]. Corb was asked to design the façade of the building in any way he liked, but instead of concentrating on this aspect he gave it to a fellow designer, Xenakis, and spent his time on inventing a new form of light and sound show, the 'Electronic Poem'. He wrote to one of the directors of Philips:

'I shall not give your pavilion a façade, but I shall compose an Electronic Poem contained in a "bottle" . . . the Poem will be composed of pictures, coloured rhythms, music. The Electronic Poem will combine

96. Philips Pavilion, Brussels, 1958.
Hyperbolic parabolas enclose a circular 'stomach'. Entrance and exit are marked by the high points. Xenakis worked out the details of this building after sketches and models of Le Corbusier.

in a coherent whole what films, recorded music, colour, words, sound and silence have until now produced independently. The Poem will last ten minutes. It will be performed for 500 spectators at a time. The pavilion will, therefore, be a stomach assimilating 500 listener spectators, and evacuating them automatically at the end of the performance . . .'[20]

The stomach form and the expressive hyperbolic-parabolas which lean away from each other in a soaring balance were the main aesthetic decisions taken by Le Corbusier and then delegated to Xenakis. One should not underrate the innovation in handling this exterior form – no architect since Gaudi had distorted mathematical and structural curves in such an expressive way – but the combination of existing sensory technologies in a new art form was the more significant contribution. Four hundred amplifiers distributed sound around the interior shells to create, along with the projected images, an intense spatial movement. These images, following each other in rapid succession, were projected all around the spectators much as later light and sound shows were to do at the World Fairs in Montreal and Tokyo. Le Corbusier spent most of his design time at various museums collecting these images. They varied

97. Philips Pavilion, 'Electronic Poem'.

in sequence from the terrifying to the harmonious, from photos of concentration camps to popular monsters to Le Corbusier's designs for communal living [97]. The music, or rather three-dimensional sound

165

arrangement, was conceived by Edgar Varèse as well as Xenakis. The total effect, a bombarding of several senses by sound, colour, light and moving images, was both backward-looking to the *Gesämtkunstwerk* of the opera, and forward-looking to the electronic media environments which Marshall McLuhan was to analyse. It did achieve the simultaneous involvement of almost all the senses and did force the spectators to participate in integrating and interpreting the evidence 'all at once', rather than in a controlled, linear sequence. The Electronic Poem, however, was the single excursion of Le Corbusier into this new medium and afterwards he returned to painting, writing and architecture.

Le Corbusier's last exhibition structure and, in fact, his final building, was his most convincing essay in lightweight technology.[21] It is a mark of his creative strength that he could produce in his middle seventies such an original and, in the context of his total *œuvre*, unusual building. In many ways the Centre Le Corbusier in Zurich is a new departure, the opening up of a new steel aesthetic [98]. In fact it does hark back to previous exhibition schemes and the pervasive ocean liner metaphor, but in terms of its lightness and erector-set aesthetic, its thin, bolted steel sections and crisp infill panels, it represents quite a new alternative to the concrete aesthetic of massive volumes set in opposition.

That this building was ever completed was due to the perseverance of Heidi Weber, an energetic, idealistic and attractive Swiss woman. A typical Corb client, she is also in some ways a precursor of Women's Lib, fighting a series of battles with the male authorities of Zurich. A self-made woman, who started off selling modern furniture, she has had to fight an assorted package of male prejudices: the Zurich planning officials, the local engineers who thought the building unsafe and even the 'so-called "Zurich Le Corbusier friends" who have harmed my activities during the realization of this Centre by uttering envious calumnies'.[22] Apparently, these last named speculated immodestly on her relation with Le Corbusier (whose wife had just died) and questioned her motives for building such a monument with which she was so closely identified in the inception and daily running. The battle continued. In 1971, she threatened to unbolt this 'flexible' building and re-erect it in another city where it was wanted, because the Town Council of Zurich would not help pay expenses for exhibitions and were only interested in obtaining the building, at its original cost, as a tourist monument for the city. Whatever its future may be, the building is now an elegant, wiry masterpiece, a sharp, witty instrument strung as tight as a harp and as light as a bow.

98. Centre Le Corbusier, Zurich 1963–7. A grey steel roof, a giant *brise-soleil*, hovers over a light steel cage filled with coloured enamel panels and clear glass.

The two sheet metal parasols hover over the steel cage with a certain tautness, being supported only at their mid-points and having expanding and diminishing sections which answer each other in antiphony: one rises, the other falls [99]. Below this basic overall theme, there is a staccato of coloured panels, steel sections and bolts. This flexible cage is constructed on Le Corbusier's favourite modulor dimension of 226 cm., the height of a man to his outstretched hand. The grid of space is carried throughout, even where there is double-height space [100], and constructed from four steel L-sections which are bolted together to form a cruciform column. This method of construction allows a great flexibility in exhibition use, the partitions and space being malleable for each new show. Twenty thousand screws were used to obtain this flexibility, and as Heidi Weber said, 'All these numerous screws created a great problem particularly in the mind of some Swiss engineers.'

The overpowering feeling is of being on a beached ship. The steel roof is painted a battleship grey; the metal doors have semicircular openings

167

99a, b, c. **Centre Le Corbusier,** various views and detail of the bolted L-sections and panels.

like the hatches of a ship; the 'top deck' of the Centre is punctuated by steel ladders and periscope holes; and finally, the main double-height exhibition space with its open staircase, metal decking and funnel is very much like the boiler room of an ocean liner [**100**]. On the exterior, the brightly coloured panels, alternating like semaphore flags, complete the metaphor and all one has to do is change the surrounding verdure to blue in order to see this building as some unusual vessel ploughing over the water. As at Ronchamp, the suggested images seem appropriate to the function. An exhibition pavilion is plausibly 'pure, neat, clear, clean and healthy', the way Le Corbusier celebrated the qualities of ocean liners.

168

oo. Centre Le Corbusier, main
xhibition space.

The several architectural languages that Le Corbusier developed are, in a way, as disarming for the critic or historian as the various messages he communicated with them. One is bound to be wrong, or at least too limited, in any attempt to summarize or fix his essential contribution. The interpretations which have been offered are either contradicted by Le Corbusier's supremely dialectical development, or they pale beside the creative wealth of his output, or they are inadequate to the curious and profound meaning of his work. One approaches it rather like the work of Shakespeare, dwarfed by its magnitude and aware that any interpretation one offers will probably extend an already embarrassingly large list of misinterpretations. The 'real' Le Corbusier is just as reluctant to stand up and give over his secret as the 'real' Hamlet. Nevertheless clues are there.

Several of the critics and detractors have tried to fix his message by excluding its richness. For instance a psychoanalyst, and also the critics Paul and Percival Goodman, try to argue that Le Corbusier was a Calvinist, a Puritan, who took too narrow a view of man and was unconcerned with the sexual dimension.[23] This interpretation, while plausible if one concentrates on the 'sterile, white boxes', simply dissolves on familiarity with the painting, Ronchamp and his sensual formalism (to say nothing of his private life). Perhaps a sensual Calvinist, or passionate Puritan, might be adequate labels, but this just shows again his dialectical richness. Other critics, especially city planning theorists such as Jane Jacobs, have faulted Le Corbusier for taking an over-simplistic view of the way the city functions, dividing it up into rigid statistical categories and paying no attention to complex, individual processes.[24] Partly this is a fair criticism but again it misses the richness and wealth of detail which he would develop when actually executing a project. Le Corbusier had the unusual ability of staying in touch with creative ideas and, judging by his Venice Hospital scheme which he was working on when he died and which has many of the complex, urban aspects which his critics were asking for, he would have changed tack once more. His creative acuity and ability to respond to new situations were shown when he sided with the younger generation of CIAM against the older, his own generation.

'[The younger group, he wrote to CIAM in 1956, were] the only ones capable of feeling actual problems, personally, profoundly . . . They are in the know. Their predecessors no longer are, they are out, they are no longer subject to the direct impact of the situation.'[25]

This cutting away of friendships and previous ideological commitments in favour of creativity and relevance were typical. The moment he felt the ideals he had fought for were anachronistic, or that his followers had betrayed him by imitation, or that other modern architects were becoming slack, he would disown them just as he had rejected his teacher L'Eplattenier or his cohort Ozenfant. The ability to burn what he loved in order to start afresh remained to the end and it is this flexibility which makes one believe that, given time, he would have answered most criticism with new developments. Indeed it is this flexibility which makes most criticisms rebound on the critic. When Lewis Mumford every so often attacked him as a 'crippled genius' who had 'warped the work of a whole generation, giving it arbitrary directives, superficial slogans, and sterile goals' – the accusation refused to stick and reflected back on the accuser, implicitly questioning his counter-values.[26] Are the British New Towns which Mumford defends any better than the Radiant City? Perhaps the Greenwich Village of Jane Jacobs and the 'organic' city of Christopher Alexander *are* better alternatives, but neither Jacobs nor Alexander is a fully committed architect who has promulgated effectively her or his values toward actualization and tested their faults. More important, it is likely that given Le Corbusier's creative flexibility, he would have come round to their views had he lived. The point worth stressing at a time when his particular ideas are so open to criticism (as the next successful ones will soon be) is that his approach remained malleable and committed to a profoundly unique view of the human condition.

It seems to me that the criticisms which are partially valid against Le Corbusier are those ostensibly based on taste. It makes sense to attack him for not providing warmth and physical lightness in a building, if that's what one wants or if the building task demands it. For instance, his Venice Hospital scheme [101] has all the heroic qualities of calmness, isolation and pure form when patients would seem to need comforting qualities of human contact and variety. But obviously this depends on the patient, his condition and taste. No clear-cut answers will ever be achieved about the ultimate appropriateness of metaphors, and one epoch's disdain for an 'heroic' hospital conceived with the Parthenon spirit will turn into another's appreciation for these qualities. This is why the idiosyncratic condemnations of Salvador Dali have a certain relevance. They are so clearly based on personal taste that, just like Le Corbusier's preferences, they can be accepted or rejected as a matter of aesthetic choice, and the lightheartedness of a joke.

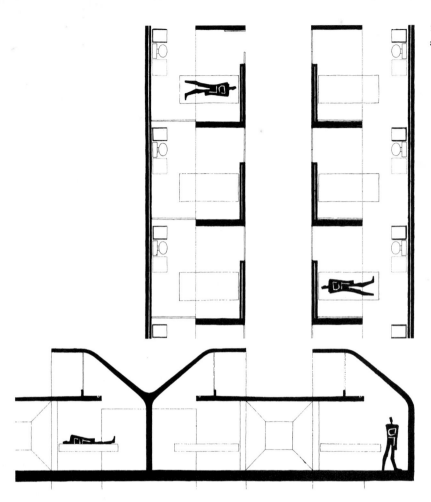

101. Venice Hospital scheme, section and plan, 1965.

'Karl Marx suffered from the same kind of illusions as poor Le Corbusier, whose recent death filled me with immense joy. Both of them were architects. Le Corbusier was a pitiable creature working in reinforced concrete. Mankind will soon be landing on the moon, and just imagine: that buffoon claimed we'd be taking along sacks of reinforced concrete. His heaviness and the heaviness of the concrete deserve one another ... Le Corbusier simply went down for the third time [when he drowned in 1965], because of his reinforced concrete and his architectures, the ugliest and most unacceptable buildings in the world. All the same, if God exists, He'd expect me to act like a gentleman. So I ordered some everlasting flowers for the anniversary of his death, next year, and I cried out: "Long live anti-gravitation." '[27] [102]

The relevance of this is its gratuity and therefore freedom of application.
If one hates reinforced concrete, or 'machines for living in', or pavilions
which look like ships, then one can choose other materials and metaphors.
The invention of and reaction to such metaphors is spontaneous and in
that sense gratuitous. It is, however, true that ultimately these metaphors
lead to deeply held values and here questions of taste become questions
about living and one's view of the human condition. It is these areas that
many people are probing when they attack Le Corbusier's architecture.
What were his ultimate values?

The answer to this is, as I have already suggested, extremely difficult
because of the plenitude of values and the fact that he constantly hid his
personal life and opinions behind a mask - the third person singular 'Le

173

Corbusier', or his various other pseudonyms. So enigmatic and veiled was his character that Maurice Besset, a friend, historian and director of the Fondation Le Corbusier, could write a book, *Who Was Le Corbusier?*, and give up the hope of an answer by the end of the introduction – an outcome which if inconsistent with respect to his title is at least wise for its humility.[28] Perhaps if one is to get close to Le Corbusier's character, it will be through a metaphorical analysis of his buildings, since these were so personally conceived as to be almost self-portraits, and an analysis of the metaphors he applied to himself.

The building that functionally comes closest to realizing his ideal of the relation between the individual and the collective is the Monastery of La Tourette located near Lyon on a sloping hill at the edge of a small forest. The violent, almost hostile, forms of one hundred monks' cells perched above a chaotic nature, defensive, aloof, withdrawn and yet unequivocally bold [103], recall the photographic portraits of Le

103. **La Tourette,** from the south-west. Horizontal layers (containing an open roof cloister, monks' cells, classrooms, library, and refectory) spill down the side of the slope.

Corbusier: implacable, stern and still sensual [23]. This building teeters on the side of a hill and the edge of verdure; it stands awkwardly and heroically apart from nature much as a Greek temple proclaiming man's loneliness and independence from the cosmos. The temple on a rugged hill, the fortress monastery closed in on itself, are both forms which emphasize man's discontinuity with nature and one should see La Tourette as the antithesis of organic architecture and its metaphors of growth, harmony, reconciliation and picturesque compromise. La Tourette's relation to nature is cataclysmic, abrupt and sublime, not harmonious: one stumbles on glimpses of the landscape framed by a violent polyphony of forms [104]. Even in the refectory, the heart of the

94 La Tourette, view of distant
landscape between a blank wall, bridge,
smoke stack and light 'canons'.

monastery where the monks take part in the good, simple life which the young Jeanneret so much admired at Mount Athos, the view over nature is disturbing and awe-inspiring, not peaceful [105]. However, one does find in this room the feeling of a simple harmony which Le Corbusier believed was the 'heroism of everyday life'. Simple, mass-produced objects, a wine flask and plates on a table, good basic food,

105. La Tourette, refectory. Brutally clear forms in precise relation. The monks eat in silence; otherwise these sharp reflective surfaces would be impossible. Note the '*ondulatoires*'.

shelter with a view of greenery and the syncopated rhythm of the *ondulatoires* – does one really need more, when these essential qualities are provided so straightforwardly? Le Corbusier actually lived much of his life like a monk [8] and thereby could see the poetry inherent in such simple objects long after they had lost their charm for other modern architects and, for that matter, the public. What had been largely a matter of taste, sophistication and fashion, the spartan aesthetic of the heroic period, was for Le Corbusier a metaphysical principle based on the universal and archetypal. Hence while many people would see his architecture and equipment as empty, dull and impoverished, he would see them as full-blown and evocative. This ambivalence is nowhere more striking than at La Tourette. Long empty corridors containing just radiators, doors and brightly painted water pipes are both dull *and* extraordinarily dramatic [106]. The Dominican monks will take you

106. **La Tourette,** corridor to offices and classrooms.

through these corridors, pointing out the changes in light, the sudden glimpses of nature and the way all the forms move in relationship as one walks. The monks have not been preconditioned as guides; they are simply perfect Corb clients responding as he would. The interior of the church, which to a layman might be a shoddily constructed, blank box, is to the monks and Le Corbusier the essence of 'ineffable space', light, calm, proportion and stark forms in tight relation [107]. One can see this space as befitting both a monk and a hero, a misanthrope and a prophet, and it is not surprising that Le Corbusier often characterized himself as an outcast or as an animal that has been kicked around. What is surprising is the occasion on which he would use these frequent self-deprecating metaphors.

For instance when he received the Royal Institute of British Architects Royal Gold Medal in 1953, he spent his entire address recounting one bitter failure after another, referring to himself as a 'true cab-horse who had received many blows with a whip'.[29] In other contexts, he referred to himself as a rat, a person who had led a dog's life, an acrobat and a clown. The image of a social outcast and beaten yet spirited animal obsessed him. When one of the CIAM architects called him a genius, he made a drawing of a bird on the back of an ass and vice-versa, saying 'Does the genius support the ass or does the ass support the genius?'[30] Here one finds the implacably honest gaze which usually criticized the world turned in on itself in lacerating self-hatred. One of his favourite books was *Don Quixote*, and no doubt he often saw himself and Pierre Jeanneret as this knight errant and Sancho Panza, tilting away at windmills in a comically pathetic rather than tragic life. Yet at other moments it was Nietzsche and a tragic struggle which were credible.

'Painting is a bitter struggle, terrifying, pitiless, unseen: a duel between the artist and himself. The struggle goes on inside, hidden on the surface. If the artist tells, he is betraying himself! . . .'[31]

There is a curiosity involved in this presentation of struggle which should not escape notice. An architect, by profession, has to inspire confidence in his clients and appear as a reasonable mediator who can get along with all sorts of people. When architects write about their work, they usually suppress any signs of conflict and try to appear as easy-going as your friendly bank manager. The reverse is true of Le Corbusier. He would actually do everything to erode confidence and increase conflict, from presenting his plans in an unconventional way to insulting his client. The logic behind this was twofold. It would disqualify at an early stage all

clients who were unwilling to accept his genius and, more importantly, allow him to present conflict as the essential quality to creative life. How else explain the fact that he would publish his unrealized projects with the condemnation of the enemy alongside them, *where they could do great damage.* His rejected Paris plans of 1937 had the following caption:

' " A megalomania worse than Ledoux's, a vandalism unique in history, the dreary uniformity, vanity and monotony of these skyscrapers ... have been proved spiritually and materially injurious, a contempt for historic and artistic tradition." (The author forgot to sign himself! ... .)'[32]

In a subconscious sense he might have felt these strictures were partially true. In any case the truth of conflict was as important as the truth of his projects and one can get an idea of the joyful bitterness with which he relates his sufferings. The following quotes are taken from various sources, but they give an idea of the pleasure he got from dramatizing struggle (including even the pleasure of identifying himself with Hamlet).

'Mr Lemaresquier points out, "This scheme [for the League of Nations] has not been drawn in Indian Ink. It breaks the rules. I insist that it should be disqualified ..." and it was ... seven schemes for Algiers rejected, unpaid ... Plans for Algiers, Stockholm, Moscow, Buenos Aires, Montevideo, Rio de Janeiro, Paris (without a break between 1912–1960), Zurich, Antwerp, Barcelona, New York, Bogotá, Saint-Dié, La Rochelle-Pallice, Marseille up to (but excluding) Chandigarh ... 1932–1935 and 1937, years of misery and of abject, blind folly by the profession and officials responsible ... But, by the autumn of 1939, Adolf Hitler was threatening Paris. The rest is silence ... Unité, 1945. Five years of storm, spite and uproar followed, despicable, ugly ... [Chandigarh 1951] is a contribution adjusted to human scale – to human size and dignity – by the efforts of a few men of character, worn, chafed and buffeted by the shocks and frictions of human relations, by the clash of individual personalities and temperaments. So be it! ... In 1956 L-C was asked to accept membership of the Institut de France [Académie des Beaux-Arts] in Paris: "Thank you, never! ... my name would serve as a banner to conceal the present evolution of the École des Beaux Arts towards a superficial modernism." '[33]

This triumphant exhilaration in defeat brings up the odd comment that it would have been a disaster had Le Corbusier always been accepted by society and been cheated of the tragic role. This tragic view challenges the major, if unconscious, assumption that positive human values are

107a, b. La Tourette, church interior with focus on the High Altar; individual altars are under the 'light canons' to the left.

realizable without extreme struggle and bitter attack. Le Corbusier accepted struggle as the very essence of men's plurality and, except that he considered warfare as barbaric, admired the courage and heroism of warriors in a way which was common in the ancient world. It is worth recalling his Nietzschean rhetoric at the age of twenty-one.

'I want to fight with truth itself. It will surely torment me. But I am not looking for quietude, or recognition from the world. I will live in sincerity, happy to undergo abuse.'[34]

In short, he brought about in his life the very bitter-sweet, tragic struggle he was looking for from the start. Judged by worldly standards his life was anything but a failure, even including the rejected schemes as failures, but judged in larger terms it was not a success. He did not realize one city plan, even Chandigarh, that brought the harmony to modern life for which he was struggling. That he dedicated himself to searching for this harmony is beyond dispute. Hence his life was ultimately a failure and judging by many late bitter comments he knew it to be one. Yet even granting this defeat as real and completely accepted, there remains the tone of indestructible joy bursting forth through the bitterness. Again it was probably Nietzsche who explained this odd duality of tragedy to Le Corbusier. In *The Birth of Tragedy*, Nietzsche focuses on the strange fact that the heroes' suffering and pain are depicted with relish and consumed by the audience with delight.[35] Why could Le Corbusier get such pleasure from his conflict and even provoke it again? Because, according to Nietzsche, the commerce with pain is metaphysical and aesthetic, not moral: it is the Dionysian ecstasy best conveyed in music and dance which asserts itself in the midst of Apollonian cerebration and reason. Whereas a reasonable approach in the face of disaster is, in the words of the engineer, 'back to the draughting board', the tragic approach is both more physical and metaphysical. On a bodily plane it is simply the resurgence of physical energy, the power of being alive, which reasserts itself independently of the mind and its worries, while on a philosophical level it grants the possibly disastrous consequences of human action no matter how well thought out and rational. The tragic view accepts and embraces this outcome with indestructible joy.

To summarize then, how far did Le Corbusier present a tragic view through his life and architecture?

On an existential level, he seems to have continually cut himself away from his friends and society, rejecting them much as a figure in tragic drama, in order to realize his own individualized view of truth. He would periodically fire members of his *atelier*, he would attack and leave his closest teachers such as L'Eplattenier and Ozenfant, he would say 'burn what you loved and love what you burned',[36] he would constantly battle with the authorities as well as with his comrades in arms such as Gropius. Why all this struggle? First, because it was exhilarating, and second, because as with Nietzsche's Superman, the creator had to master his opponents' power, their ideas, before he would go on to destroy them in order to re-create them in a new synthesis. This destructive-constructive pattern is perhaps as common to the creative temperament as it is to the tragic figure in western drama, and Nietzsche's Superman is in part like the archetypal scientist as much as the tragic hero trying to restructure social values. But whereas the scientist re-examines and re-constitutes existing patterns to build new theories, the tragic hero reinvents them for this and another reason: in order to present a truth about the world and about the individual's suffering in solitude ' . . . Art is a deep love of one's ego, which one seeks in retreat and solitude, this divine ego which can be a terrestrial ego when it is forced by a struggle to become so . . . It is in solitude that one can struggle with one's ego, that one punishes and encourages oneself'.[36] Here the young Jeanneret of twenty-one sounds like both the prophet in the wilderness and the typical figure of modern tragedy, Hamlet, dramatizing his doubts and sufferings – even his loneliness. Again this loneliness may be common to both creator and tragic hero since they both have to abandon the ordinary conventions of society. But the tragic hero accentuates his loneliness as a main theme in the drama – we attend his soliloquies, his tortured, inward questionings, as much as the unfolding of events.

It seems to me Le Corbusier's writings and architecture also dramatize this loneliness and suffering. For instance the church and corridors of La Tourette [106] are positively empty. The blank surfaces are not just an absence of conventional symbolism, but a very strong symbol in their own right. The feeling one has in much of Le Corbusier's architecture is of being dramatically isolated in a beautiful but hostile cosmos – like, for instance, walking in the Grand Canyon or on a desolate Greek mountain range without the comforts, noise or familiarity of daily life. The forms are brutal and harsh, sometimes even tortured [102] – the bell 'tower' of La Tourette perches anxiously, even awkwardly, over the church, at once a metaphor for the Church's insecurity and Le Corbusier's loneliness. Most bell towers are proud, vertical and strong. This one is twice deflected, on a diagonal and it is defiant rather than secure. Perhaps it is stretching a point, but again Le Corbusier's physiognomy is there. The implacable stare of the genius combined with the bent body of the cab-horse or ass.

It is just as hard, however, with Le Corbusier's architecture, as it is with tragedy to decide ultimately whether it is suffering and loneliness which triumph, or exhilaration. Is one depressed at the end of a tragedy? If so it is a strange kind of depression which seems robbed of its finality. Somehow the idealistic action of the tragic hero cheats his defeat of its ultimate pain. Le Corbusier continually tried to realize his goal of 'harmony' for an industrial civilization, but was repulsed so often that his incessant efforts appear to be literally mad, insane, pragmatically futile. What was the meaning of an idealism which would only fail again? Perhaps symbolic. Perhaps Le Corbusier, like the tragic hero, saw the conflict between his ideals and society as being of equal importance as the attainment of these ideals. He certainly enjoyed these conflicts. And he presented 'joy' in many key parts of a building: the 'three essential joys', sun, space and greenery; the colour and crisp materials which would contrast with brutal concrete. Everywhere the message is mixed, just as the meaning of tragedy is dualistic. One can see this dualism in a drawing which Le Corbusier produced while he was struggling with the authorities over the Unité at Marseille. It is a double portrait, perhaps of himself: part Apollo, part Medusa, part the smiling sun god of reason, part the Dionysian, sensual figure of the underworld – a dark bitterness just barely balanced by joy and light [108].

108. Sketch, 1945.

Notes

INTRODUCTION

1. Peter Smithson, 'Mies is Great but Corb Communicates', *Architectural Association Journal,* May 1959.

CHAPTER 1: JEANNERET'S SCHOOL FOR LE CORBUSIER 1887–1916

1. *The Radiant City*, New York, 1967, pp. 192–3; first published as *La Ville Radieuse*, Paris, 1935.

2. Quoted from Geoffrey Hellman profile, 'From Within to Without', in the *New Yorker Magazine*, 26 April and 3 May 1947.

3. *L'Art décoratif d'aujourd'hui*, Paris, 1925, p. 198. The early buildings have been published by Etienne Chavanne and Michel Laville in *Werk*, December 1965, pp. 483–8.

4. *Towards a New Architecture*, trans. from the French by Frederick Etchells. First published in England 1927 by John Rodker. The Architectural Press facsimile edition 1946, 1948, 1952, 1956, 1959, 1963, 1965. First paperback edition 1970. Etchells's translation of 1927 made from 13th French edition. Book originally published in Paris in 1923 by Éditions Crès under title *Vers une Architecture*, from articles appearing in *L'Esprit Nouveau* since October 1920.

5. Paul Turner, 'The Education of Le Corbusier – a Study of the Development of Le Corbusier's Thought, 1900–1920', unpublished Ph.D. thesis, Harvard University, April 1971; Henry Provensal, *L'Art de demain*, Paris, 1904, p. 145. The quote is taken from Paul Turner's article 'The Beginnings of Le Corbusier's Education, 1902–07', *The Art Bulletin*, 53, June, 1971, p. 221. The notion of ideal beauty Provensal probably got from Julien Guadet's *Elements et théories de l'architecture*, I, 99, as Turner points out.

6. Paul Turner's *Art Bulletin* Article, p. 215, shows the influence of the French Art Nouveau designers on Jeanneret at this time.

7. It is worth noting that while Jeanneret did reject *decorative* motifs after this year, he always kept a high regard for rhythmical *ornament* – that is 'an elevated conception of ornament . . . conceived of as a microcosm'. This distinction between decoration and ornament is crucial for the later Le Corbusier, who spurned all decoration and derived ornament from structure and construction.

8. Letter from Charles-Édouard Jeanneret to Charles L'Eplattenier, Paris, 22 November 1908, *Aujourd'hui Art et Architecture*, November 1965, p. 10.

9. Le Corbusier, *Précisions sur un état présent de l'architecture et de l'urbanisme*, Paris, 1930, pp. 17–18.

10. Charles-Édouard Jeanneret, letter, 1908, op. cit.

11. See Paul Turner's thesis, op. cit. Turner has looked very closely at the books Jeanneret collected and annotated up to 1930 and has established that Jeanneret read *Zarathustra* about 1908. My own previous research had established a general link between Nietzsche and Le Corbusier and also his dualism based on this link. See my 'Charles Jeanneret – Le Corbusier', *Arena*, May 1967, in its revised form as part of my Ph.D. thesis 'Modern Architecture since 1945', London University, 1970. There I discuss the influence of Hegel and Nietzsche's *The Birth of Tragedy*. It seems to me he understood Nietzsche's ideas as I argue in conclusion.

12. Charles-Édouard Jeanneret, letter, 1908, op. cit.

13. ibid., but the following Wednesday, 25 November 1908.

14. *Towards a New Architecture*, p. 24.

15. Charles-Édouard Jeanneret, *Étude sur le mouvement d'art décoratif en Allemagne*, La Chaux-de-Fonds, 1912. The influence of the Garden City movement on Le Corbusier can be found in Brian B. Taylor, *Le Corbusier et Pessac 1914–1928*, Vols. 1 and 2, Paris, 1972.

16. Paul Turner, Ph.D. thesis, op. cit., p. 80.

17. Quoted from Maurice Besset, *Who Was Le Corbusier?*, Geneva, 1968, p. 11, and Le Corbusier, *My Work*, London, 1960, p. 37.

18. Le Corbusier, *Entretien avec les étudiants des écoles d'architecture*, Paris, 1943, translated as *Talks with Students*, New York, 1961, p. 77.

19. Charles Jeanneret, *Le Voyage d'Orient*, written 1911–14, re-edited by Le Corbusier on 17 July 1965, and published Meaux, 1966, p. 38.

20. ibid., p. 154.

21. *Towards a New Architecture*, p. 190.

22. ibid., pp. 195, 197, 201.

23. ibid., pp. 202–4.

24. Jean Petit, *Le Corbusier Lui-Même*, Geneva, 1970, p. 45. The source and date of this quote are not given by Petit.

25. See Paul Turner's thesis. Turner argues that Jeanneret was the principle author of this document, because its style is similar to the later polemical writings of Le Corbusier.

26. Jean Petit, op. cit., p. 489, quoted from *La Sentinelle*, La Chaux-de-Fonds, 1 December 1916.

27. See Hugh Honour, *Neo-classicism*, Penguin Books, Harmondsworth, 1968, pp. 129–30, for Goethe's *Altar of Good Fortune*, which like much neo-classicism seems to have been an inspiration for 'modern' architecture.

28. Jean Petit, op. cit., p. 46. Letter from La Chaux-de-Fonds dated 28 October 1915.

1. *L'Art décoratif d'aujourd'hui*, p. 217.

2. Amédée Ozenfant, *Mémoirs 1886-1962*, Paris, 1968, quoted from *Aujourd'hui Art et Architecture*, November 1965, pp. 14-15. The first date of meeting is disputed. Le Corbusier claimed it was a year later, in the spring of 1918.

3. Charles Jeanneret and Amédée Ozenfant, *Après le Cubisme*, Paris, 1918.

4. ibid., also quoted in *Aujourd'hui Art et Architecture*, pp. 14-15.

5. Paul Turner in his thesis comes to much the same conclusions on who wrote most of which chapters, from the internal evidence and style. The interest in comparing the 'rigour' of the Parthenon with that of the machine was more Le Corbusier's than Ozenfant's.

6. *Towards a New Architecture*, p. 210.

7. 'Le Purisme', *L'Esprit Nouveau*, 4, 1921, pp. 369-86, quoted from Robert L. Herbert, *Modern Artists on Art*, Englewood Cliffs, New Jersey, 1964, pp. 61-2.

8. *Aujourd'hui Art et Architecture*, p. 15.

9. Quoted from Geoffrey Hellman, op. cit.

10. Le Corbusier, *The Four Routes*, London, 1947, p. 103; written in French as *Sur les 4 Routes*, Paris, 1941.

11. *L'Art décoratif d'aujourd'hui*. The apology was written at the re-edition of the book in 1959, p. xv.

12. Le Corbusier-Saugnier, *L'Esprit Nouveau*, 9, 1922(?).

13. ibid.

14. *L'Esprit Nouveau*, 19, 1923.

15. Paul Boulard, *L'Esprit Nouveau*, 25, 1925.

16. ibid.

17. *L'Art décoratif d'aujourd'hui*, p. 17.

18. *Towards a New Architecture*, p. 17.

19. ibid., p. 17.

20. ibid., p. 23.

21. ibid., p. 23.

22. ibid., pp. 192-6.

23. ibid., p. 22.

24. ibid., p. 96.

25. ibid., p. 126.

26. ibid., p. 142.

27. ibid., pp. 258-9.

28. Le Corbusier, *The City of Tomorrow*, trans. Frederick Etchells, London, 1929, p. 7, from *Urbanisme*, Paris, 1925. As Reyner Banham has pointed out, the pack-donkey also walks in a straight line - if given a flat surface and a big push.

29. ibid., p. 38.

30. ibid., p. 74.

31. ibid., pp. 298-301.

32. Le Corbusier and Pierre Jeanneret, *Oeuvre Complète, Volume I, 1910-1929*, ed. W. Boesiger and O. Stonorov, Geneva, 1929, p. 78.

33. Quoted from Philippe Boudon's excellent sociological study, *Pessac de le Corbusier*, Paris, 1969, p. 11.

34. *The City of Tomorrow*, p. 72.

35. Philippe Boudon, op. cit.

36. Ulrich Conrads, *Programmes and Manifestoes on 20th Century Architecture*, London, 1970, p. 111. The statement comes from the CIAM foundation manifesto of 1928.

37. *L'Art décoratif d'aujourd'hui*, pp. 39, 42.

38. ibid., p. 67.

39. *Towards a New Architecture*, p. 89.

40. *L'Art décoratif d'aujourd'hui*, p. 76.

41. ibid., p. 1.

42. ibid., p. 8.

43. ibid., p. 24.

44. ibid., p. 128.

45. *Towards a New Architecture*, pp. 114-15.

46. *La Peinture Moderne*, Paris, 1925, p. 37.

47. ibid., p. 138.

48. ibid., pp. 153-4.

49. ibid., pp. 170-72.

50. ibid., p. 10

51. *Oeuvre Complète, Volume I, 1910-1929*, p. 128-9.

52. *Towards a New Architecture*, p. 114.

CHAPTER 3: AT WAR WITH REACTION 1928-45

1. Quoted from memory by Kunio Maekawa, the Japanese architect who worked with Le Corbusier, in *Aujourd'hui Art et Architecture*, op. cit. p. 109.

2. Jean Petit, *Le Corbusier Lui-Même*, p. 77.

3. Taya Zinkin, 'No Compromise with Corbusier', *Guardian*, 11 September 1965.

4. Jean Petit, op. cit., pp. 120-21 and Le Corbusier, *My Work*, p. 199.

5. Jean Petit, op. cit., p. 68.

6. Taya Zinkin, op. cit.

7. Le Corbusier, *When the Cathedrals were White, a Journey to the Country of Timid People*, New York, 1947 (written in 1935 and 1945), pp. 135-6.

8. ibid., p. 137.

9. ibid., p. 145.

10. ibid., pp. 146-7.

11. ibid., pp. 150-51.

12. ibid., p. 151.

13. Le Corbusier, *The Radiant City*, p. 6.

14. Le Corbusier, *My Work*, p. 86.

15. Le Corbusier and Pierre Jeanneret, *Oeuvre Complète, Volume I, 1910-1929*, p. 190.

16. Le Corbusier, *The Radiant City*, p. 200.

17. ibid., p. 186.

18. Le Corbusier, *When the Cathedrals were White*, pp. 5, 4.

19. Le Corbusier, *The Radiant City*, p. 177-9.

20. Le Corbusier, *When the Cathedrals were White*, p. 168.

21. Quoted by Lionel March in a review of Norma Evenson's book, *Le Corbusier, the Machine and the Grand Design*, in *Design* magazine, 1970, p. 70.

22. Some of this material I covered in *Architecture 2000 - Predictions and Methods*, London, 1971 - the section called 'La Trahison perpétuelle des clercs' which was slightly expanded in *Archithese II*, Zurich, fall 1971. Further references can be found there, although the overall problem has not been adequately dealt with anywhere.

23. Jean Petit, op. cit., p. 75, and *Oeuvre Complète, Volume II, 1929-34*, pp. 17-18.

24. For these arguments and much else of biographical interest see Maximilien Gauthier's war-time biography, *Le Corbusier ou L'architecte au service de l'homme*, Paris, 1944, the section on '*Le Cheval de Troie du Bolchevisme*', pp. 176-98.

25. Jean Petit, op. cit., p. 81.

26. ibid., p. 78. The 'other story' was told to me by M. Andrieni at the Foundation le Corbusier.

27. Le Corbusier, *Précisions*, pp. 96-7.

28. Jean Petit, op. cit., p. 87.

29. Le Corbusier, *My Work*, p. 147.

30. Geoffrey Hellman, op. cit.

31. Hannah Arendt, 'Bertolt Brecht', in *Men in Dark Times*, London, 1970, pp. 207-50.

CHAPTER 4: OTHER LANGUAGES OF ARCHITECTURE 1946-65

1. Le Corbusier, *When the Cathedrals Were White*, pp. 103-4.

2. For these ideas see Peter Serenyi, 'Le Corbusier, Fourier and the Monastery of Ema', in *Art Bulletin*, December 1967; also Le Corbusier, *The Marseilles Block*, London, 1953.

3. Le Corbusier, *Le Voyage d'Orient*, p. 154.

4. Peter Blake, *Le Corbusier*, Penguin Books, Harmondsworth, 1963, p. 123.

5. Le Corbusier, *Oeuvre Complète, Volume V, 1946–52*, p. 191.

6. ibid., p. 191.

7. Jean Petit, *Le Corbusier Lui-Même*, p. 122.

8. Le Corbusier, *My Work*, p. 138.

9. Constantinos Nivola, *Architectural Forum*, December 1969, p. 60.

10. Le Corbusier, *The New World of Space*, New York, 1948, p. 8.

11. The two main attacks were James Stirling's 'Le Corbusier's Chapel and the Crisis of Rationalism', in *Architectural Review*, March 1956, pp. 155–61, and Nikolaus Pevsner's *An Outline of European Architecture*, Penguin Books, Harmondsworth, 1963, p. 429. There were other attacks by critics such as G. C. Argan which typified the attitude of a whole generation of architects brought up on the tenets of rationalism.

12. Le Corbusier, *Oeuvre Complète, Volume V, 1946–52*, p. 72.

13. Le Corbusier, *The Chapel at Ronchamp*, London, 1957, p. 7.

14. See Noam Chomsky, *Syntactic Structures,* The Hague, 1957; *Language and Mind*, New York, 1968.

15. Regrettably I have lost the source of this quote.

16. See above, p. 86.

17. Said often by Le Corbusier, for instance in *L'Art décoratif d'aujourd'hui*, p. 217.

18. Stanilaus von Moos shows the transposition of forms from one function to another in *Le Corbusier, l'architecte et son Mythe*, France, 1971, pp. 132–5.

19. An incomplete list of the 'words' or invented signs: 1. Domino structure; 2. pilotis; 3. roof garden; 4. free plan; 5. ribbon window; 6. free façade; 7. cell-box; 8. empty wall; 9. slab block; 10. zig-zag blocks; 11. serpentine slab; 12. loggia niche; 13. picture wall; 14. movable partitions; 15. curved wall; 16. interior ramps; 17. pivoting doors; 18. neutralizing wall; 19. double height space; 20. undulating roof; 21. independent roof; 22. sculpture on roof; 23. exhaust stacks; 24. rain spouts; 25. spiral stair; 26. bare stair; 27. *ondulatoires*; 28. *brises-soleil*; 29. bottle rack; 30. cooling towers; 31. Spiral Museum; 32. light catchers; 33. tapering pilotis; 34. *béton brut*; 35. 4 Functions; 36. 3 Essential Joys; 37. 7 V's – Circulation Separation; 38. 6 Shades; 39. Regulating lines and Modulor; 40. tension cants at Firminy.

20. Le Corbusier, *My Work*, p. 186.

21. This was the final work which he saw through to the working drawing stage; there were other works, completed after his death, in Chandigarh, Firminy, etc. The projects that influenced the Zurich Pavilion were his Nestlé building of 1928 and pavilions for Liège, 1937, and Tokyo, 1957.

22. Heidi Weber, *Documentation of the Centre Le Corbusier*, Zurich, 1967, p. 7.

23. For the attacks on Le Corbusier as a sexual puritan see Gaston Bardot, 'Charles-Édouard contre Le Corbusier, Essai de Psychoanalyse', in *Revue de Mediterranée*, September – December 1947, pp. 513–30, 682–96; and Paul and Percival Goodman, *Communitas*, New York, 1960, p. 49.

24. Jane Jacobs, *The Death and Life of Great American Cities*, New York, 1960, first and last chapters.

25. Jurgen Joedicke, *CIAM '59 in Otterlo*, London, 1961, p. 16.

26. Lewis Mumford, *Progressive Architecture*, October 1965, p. 236, and 'The Case against Modern Architecture' and 'The Marseilles Folly', in *The Highway and the City*, New York, 1963.

27. Alain Bosquet, *Conversations with Dali*, New York, 1969, pp. 16, 17, 31.

28. Maurice Besset, op. cit., pp. 7-8, 196.

29. *Royal Institute of British Architects Journal*, April 1953, p. 218.

30. Siegfried Giedion, *Space, Time and Architecture*, 5th edn, Cambridge, Mass., 1967, pp. 568-9.

31. Le Corbusier, *My Work*, p. 219.

32. ibid., p. 131.

33. ibid., pp. 49, 50, 51, 52, 138, 140, 141.

34. Charles Jeanneret, letter to Charles L'Eplattenier, 1908, op. cit.

35. Frederick Nietzsche, *The Birth of Tragedy*, trans. Francis Golffing, New York, 1956, pp. 142-3.

36. See Chapter One, note 8 for this quote, written when Jeanneret was twenty-one.

Acknowledgements for Illustrations

The photographs for this book were taken by Charles Jencks except the following:

The Architectural Press, London (*The Architectural Review*, April 1936): 54, 55; Archizoom: 39; Artemis Verlag, Zurich (Le Corbusier, *Oeuvre complète*, Volumes I–VIII): 1, 2, 3, 7, 22a, 27, 29, 32, 35, 49, 52, 57, 58, 59, 60, 61, 62, 66, 68, 70, 71, 72, 73, 75, 82, 101, 108. Alan Blanc (Courtesy of the Architectural Association): 18a. Dokumentation Le Corbusier, Stiftung Heidi Weber, Zurich: 8, 24, 50, 51, 53, 56, 63, 65a, 65b, 74, 96. Dunod, Paris *(Pessac de Le Corbusier)*, by Philippe Boudon, © Dunod 1969): 34b. Editions Crès, Paris *(Vers une architecture)*, 12, 44; *(L'Art décoratif d'aujourd'hui)*, 10, 30; *(Collection de l'Esprit Nouveau)*, 25, 28. Fondation Le Corbusier, Paris: 11, 22b, 23, 36, 38, 67, 97; French Government Tourist Office, London: 88, 89, 90; Lucien Hervé, Paris: 64; Information Service of India, London: 92a, 93b; Rhomi Khosla: 91a–f, 92b. 93a; Marseille, Unité d'Habitation, post-card, 83; Tino Nivola: 85, 86, 87; Victoria and Albert Museum, London: 37a, 37c; F. R. Yerbury (Courtesy of the Architectural Association): 31b, 34a, 41, 42, 43, 45. Unknown copyright: 26, 33, 69. Drawings by Paul White (18b, 95) and Ken Yeang (40a and b).

Index